ROUGH MAGIC

SCENES FROM AN ACTOR'S LIFE

ROUGH MAGIC

SCENES FROM AN ACTOR'S LIFE

JONATHAN GILLARD

Jonathan Gillard Daly

Jonathan Gillard Daly

Jonathan Gillard Daly

JONATHAN GILLARD DALY

Editor: Cherie Kephart
Proofreader: Paula Fitzgerald
Cover Design and Book Production: WildGraphics | asawild.org
Published by: Book Baby | bookbaby.com

Printed in the United States of America

To Anne McMahon
(1942-2022)
My big sister and unflagging supporter.
I grieve that you didn't live long
enough to read these words.

◆

To Gale, Sam, and Emily,
with love and gratitude,
always and forever.

TABLE OF CONTENTS

This rough magic I here abjure.

William Shakespeare
The Tempest, Act Five, Scene 1

PROLOGUE

(March 2020. Milwaukee, Wisconsin. Monday night—actors' night off. A hundred theater lovers are gathered in a voguish tavern on the lower East Side, despite the frigid, snowy night, to mark the retirement of the artistic director of a small but successful professional theater. A temporary stage has been erected at one end of the room. Two chairs, a couple of microphone stands, and a piano have been set up on the platform.)

(JON, a tall, thin, white-haired fellow with an air of slightly shabby elegance, is standing at the bar, having finished his beer much faster than he intended. He is part of the evening's entertainment and always feels uncomfortable mixing with an audience before he's "on." He is leaning his arm on the bar rail, trying in vain to get the attention of the bartender. A burly young man sitting at the stool next to him wipes the beer foam from his ample red beard. He'd make a good Santa Claus if he wasn't so young. He touches JON on the arm to get his attention. JON smiles stiffly.)

YOUNG SANTA
So, what's next for you?

JON
(With a vague smile)
Sorry…?

YOUNG SANTA

(Indicating his girlfriend sitting next to him)
Oh, we know you. You're the actor. We've seen you in lots of plays.

JON

Oh, you have….

YOUNG SANTA

So, what's next?

JON

I don't know, exactly.

YOUNG SANTA

Takin' a little break, are you?

JON

(His eyes searching for the bartender)
Yeah, I suppose I am.

YOUNG SANTA

(Reaching for his wallet)
What are you drinking?

JON

Thanks, but I'm just going to get some water. I've got to be on that
stage in a minute.

*(YOUNG SANTA's girlfriend cuts through the dull din with a voice
full of sunshine and fresh air. She looks like she could be at home
on a soccer field. Or a basketball court. Her bronzed arms suggest
that she spent the summer playing volleyball at the beach. SANTA'S
GIRLFRIEND is wearing bracelets on both wrists, and they jangle
and thrum, matching her extravagant gestures.)*

SANTA'S GIRLFRIEND

What you do must be so fun! I saw *Forty-Second Street* at the Skylight last week, and they looked like they were having such a great time. I wish my life was like that.

JON

Well, I wouldn't do it if it wasn't fun....

(JON groans on the inside to hear his shopworn platitude ringing in his ears. He looks to the other end of the bar and is relieved to see the guest of honor, MICHAEL, motioning him to join him in front of the platform.)

JON

(To SANTA and his girlfriend)
I'm sorry, we're about to start. It was great talking with you....

(End of scene. Thank God.)

I'VE BEEN IN THIS bar for almost an hour, wearing my public face. The muscles in my jaw are sore from overwork. The place is packed with actors filling the stale air with forced laughter, desperately projecting confidence in the face of the uncertainty that gnaws away at the psyche of every actor who ever lived. I work my way through the crowd, nodding and smiling, until I reach Michael.

He's about my age, maybe a year or two shy of my sixty-five years. He's a character actor like me, and his boundless energy and friendly vibe have served him well in his two decades as an artistic director. It's been a great run, but now he's tired. He wants to retire, maybe act in a play every so often. He's expressing his ambivalence about this farewell party with his choice of costume: sober dark-blue sport coat, screaming loud Hawaiian shirt, blue jeans, and spotless sneakers. How does he keep those things so white when he's sloshing through the slush-filled sidewalks?

For all the high energy level of the evening, he looks relaxed, like a guy who's looking forward to lounging in a deck chair with a mai tai in hand, dozing off in the sun.

He places his hand in the small of my back, like he's about to take me for a spin across the dance floor. He raises his voice just high enough so I can hear him over the din.

"This'll be no sweat, I promise. I just ask you a couple of questions, what it was like to work with me, and then you lie like a rug. How's that?"

"I won't be lying, Michael. You produced the first play I ever wrote."

"Good, we can talk about that. That'll fill the time just fine. Then we can finish up and get good and drunk."

I smile. A real smile. I'm going to miss Michael. He's a good guy. And he lives by one of my favorite principles in my *Rules for Actors*. It's my *Rule #1: Leave the drama onstage.*

Michael picks up a microphone, invites the hundred people in the room to take their seats, and we begin. I'm sitting on a hard-backed chair that makes my spine straighten. The back of the chair is already digging into my shoulder blades. I hope this doesn't take long.

Michael puts one hand in his pocket, strolling across the stage, chatting effortlessly with a roomful of friends. He's all the things a leader should be: charming, armed with a few dependable jokes, and generous with praise for his colleagues.

He faces me. "Jon, you've worked as an actor in this town for, what, twenty years? But when I first got the chance to work with you, I directed a play that you wrote. Our theme tonight is about the new plays that our theater mentored over the last decade. What was the process like for you?"

He hands me the microphone and sits in the other rickety chair.

I wish I'd prepared for this. It's been almost ten years since my play premiered here and trying to conjure up the memory of it is like rummaging through a pile of ashes. I've been on the production line for so long, churning out play after play, and there never seems to be enough time for reflection.

Well, here's your chance, Dummy. Reflect.

I bring the microphone to my mouth and begin.

"Writing a play is kind of a conversation with yourself. You have to know why you're writing it, what you want to say. And then, when you're all done, you've got to convince somebody to help you put it on stage. It's an act of faith and generosity for a colleague to recognize that what you want to say has some meaning to an audience. I'll always think of Michael as a guy who gave my play a chance to speak."

Everybody's looking at me. Michael is nodding and smiling. I'm flustered, having run out of things to say, and my unease is heating up my cheeks and my ears, as if I'm sitting in front of a bonfire.

The sound of applause assures me I'm done talking. My inner judge is already busy critiquing me.

Boy, I wish I hadn't turned down that beer.

I step off the stage, and there's a big crowd forming around the bar. It's going to take me a long time to get a drink. Is it worth the effort? I'm ready to go home. I don't think I can manage being part of a crowd anymore.

I bypass the bar, dabble in a few peremptory greetings to friends who wouldn't understand if I avoided them, and head for the door. Now I'm on a mission: to escape efficiently, without drawing any further attention to myself. I keep moving, waving to friends across the room. I hug a few people who are only distant acquaintances, just so I can ease my way forward. I chide my inner self for my arrogance, but it's getting to the point that I really want to get the hell out of here.

I shove open the door, and the frosty night air brings me to life. My car is less than a block away. The sounds of the bar fade as I walk. I tap the remote key and climb into the front seat.

With the push of the ignition button, my little subcompact hums to life. The engine sounds like a sewing machine quietly going about its business. In moments, warm air spins through the cabin.

The streets are quiet. I turn off the radio and take in the silence.

In my mind's eye, I see Michael in his deck chair, working on his second mai tai. I think about joining him.

My thoughts wander as I drive.

I'm on my way home, but where am I going?

I've always had a job on the horizon. Ninety-five percent of the last forty years I've been busily employed as a stage actor. When I turn sixty-six next month, I'll collect my first social security check. When I add that to my pension, I'll be bringing home more cash than I ever did as a working actor.

I see the streetlights hazy beneath a blanket of cold. I can no longer hear the faint drone of the car. But my thoughts get louder.

Is it time to step off the stage for good? And if I'm not acting, can I still call myself an actor?

And if I'm not an actor, who am I?

Chapter 1

MR. TWEEDY

(June 1961. Lights up on a cheery family room in Milwaukee. It's Saturday morning, and a seven-year-old boy in a white T-shirt and shorts is stretched out on the Naugahyde sofa. He is dangling his stocking feet over the end of the sofa, as his mother has instructed him. He reaches for the newspaper just as his father enters the room. DAD is dressed in his Saturday-morning lawn-mowing uniform, which is spread over his skinny frame: white shirt, thin black tie, gray pants, white parka zipped up to his sternum. His tie is unencumbered by a tie clasp. After all, it's Saturday.)

DAD

Hey, Schmidt, where are your shoes?

JON

(Rolling his eyes)

They're right here. I just took them off for a while.

DAD

What if everybody in our family did that? We'd have eight pairs of shoes all over the house. Put them on, please. But don't sit with your shoes on the couch. You'll get the cushions dirty.

(JON steps into his penny loafers with as much attitude as he can muster safely. Then he returns his attention to the morning paper.)

DAD

Careful, Son, I haven't finished reading that. What are you looking for, the Sports?

JON

The Green Sheet.

DAD

Well, go ahead. I don't read the funny papers anyway. But leave the business section where I can find it, please.

(As DAD brushes past JON on his way to the back door, JON smells something funny on DAD's breath. Mouthwash? Or that stuff in the dark-green bottle that he keeps in the cupboard over the refrigerator? DAD exits.)

EVERY SATURDAY MORNING, I started the day with the funny pages. My favorite strip was *Mr. Tweedy*—a lovable, unassuming putz with a head shaped like a cue ball, dressed in the outfit of every male office worker, circa 1961: black suit, white shirt, thin black tie, gray hat. Mister Tweedy bumbled his way through his single-paneled life, in the lower left-hand corner of the Green Sheet.

Even at seven years old, I could see myself in him. Someday I'd be in his shoes, wearing his funny clothes. My family had me destined for law or business. But like Mr. Tweedy, I felt ill-suited for a gray-flannel life.

Here was Mr. Tweedy, sitting in an office chair, holding his hat tightly in hand, with a slightly pained expression on his face captured by a wavering line to indicate the contours of his little slash of a mouth. He was being interviewed for a job by a fellow cue-ball head, his black suit jacket hanging from the back of his chair, black tie loosened, sleeves rolled to his forearms, all this indicating that he was the one in charge and Mr. Tweedy was clearly the supplicant.

I stared at the comic panel, and the characters came to life.

The Boss was pushing paper across his desk, finally coming upon Mr. Tweedy's job application.

"What can you do?" asked the Boss.

"Well, I like funny stories," replied Mr. Tweedy. "The ones that happen in a house that looks a lot like the house I live in, with a wife and a small child and nice Ethan Allen furniture. Maybe a kitchen."

"Sorry, we're all full of Dick Van Dykes right now."

"Oh, that's too bad. I was kind of hoping for a Dick Van Dyke."

"How about his brother Jerry? Do you play the banjo?"

"No."

"Or Ward Cleaver? We might have an opening for a *Leave it to Beaver*...."

"That sounds good," says Mr. Tweedy. "When do I start?"

"Ten o'clock Monday. At the studio. See you then."

In a flash, my future came into focus, like a print from a Polaroid camera, as if I'd snapped the photo, peeled back the ejected paper, lacquered it with the developing fluid, and held it out as the photo came to life. What I really wanted to be was something so crazy that I couldn't even imagine how you'd go about becoming one. Nobody in my family did this. Nobody I'd ever met did this.

I wanted to be an actor.

That way I could *pretend* to be a lawyer, or a doctor, or even a secret agent. I bet that would be even more fun than being a real one.

But how do you *become* an actor?

Simple. Being an actor is a job, right? When I grow up, I'd go to an office with lots of ringing phones and people scurrying all over the place holding on to folders stuffed with papers, and I'd tell the cue-ball head with his sleeves rolled up that I want to be an actor.

After that Saturday morning with the Green Sheet, the idea of being an actor swam around in my head like a catchy TV jingle. Every time I tuned into a sitcom or a Western or a shaving cream commercial,

I'd start dreaming of the day that I'd be in that box, doing the only thing I'd ever want to do.

Question: How do you get to be a TV star, even when you're only seven?

Rules for Actors, Rule #2: Practice.

Chapter 2

GO GET 'EM, BRAVES

THE BASEMENT OF OUR house was my hideout, my safe place, my testing ground, the entranceway into my forever dreams. It was one of those "finished" recreation rooms, with a concrete floor covered over with linoleum squares of burgundy red and amber gold. Chocolate-stained wainscotting adorned the room on three sides, and built-in cabinetry lined the fourth wall. A de-humidifier hummed along all year round. My allergy-plagued older brother could be found here just about every day in July and August, because it was the only place where his body didn't convulse into burnout from sneezing. When he wasn't holed up there, it was my studio.

The round table made of lightweight cane was the desk where I welcomed the guests on my late-night talk show. Sometimes I sat at one of the wicker chairs and chattered away to the invisible host.

"You know, Johnny, sometimes it just seems like a wonderful dream. I hope I never wake up. How could I ever have guessed that one day all this would happen to me?"

"Jon, you deserve it. Don't you think so, folks?"

(Wild applause. I wave, and then I raise my hand to quell the ovation.) *"Oh folks, you're too kind...."*

The pool table, a massive relic that my banker grandfather had bought from a beggared client during the depths of the Depression, was the kitchen counter where my TV wife (played by who else but Mary Tyler Moore?) chopped vegetables and slapped away my hand when I tried to sample the dip.

"Now, now, you'll just have to wait for dinner like everybody else."

"I can't help it, honey, I'm starving!" (*The studio audience erupts into laughter.*)

My sound system was of the highest quality: a General Electric All-in-One Monaural Home Entertainment System with a three-speed turntable, a couple of detachable box speakers with battleship-gray fabric mounted over the woofers and tweeters or whatever was in there, and all of it balanced on a deluxe aluminum platform on rollers that could be moved over the linoleum with a minimum of fuss. I spent hours every day listening to records until I had memorized the words to dozens of songs.

When I put *Meet the Beatles* on, I'd jump out of my chair and throw myself into imitating the Lads' gyrations: the boyish hoping of Paul, the brooding lurking of George, spread-legged bad boy John flaunting his crotch to the camera; and happy-go-lucky, cut-off-at-the-waist Ringo, shaking the bangs out of his face as he pounded out the beat. When each song ended, I'd take a bow as the sweat started to pool at my temples. I even provided the sounds of teenaged girls screaming their approval by placing a hissing sound at the back of my throat and pushing it forward so the sound grew into a wheeze of hysteria that would resonate through my head until I felt like I was going to faint.

And then there was Motown. The Four Tops, the Temptations. With my prepubescent voice, it was easy to reach the high croon of Sam Cooke. I screamed myself hoarse imitating the frenzied growl of Wilson Pickett, living every suburban kid's fantasy of finding the soul brother buried deep within my lily-white skin.

I sang, I drummed, I even placed myself in the horn section, pretending to howl out one of those berserk trumpet solos as all that thrilling brass surrounded me.

The only album that obsessed me even more was called *Go Get 'Em, Braves*. It was a commemorative disk that chronicled the Milwaukee

Braves' rise to glory in 1958 when they won the World Series, complete with archival recordings of the Braves' most sublime moments.

"Swing and a drive to deep left field back toward the wall.... It's back at that fence...it's going over and it's a home run! The Braves are the Champions of the National League! Holy cow!"

"Spahnie on the mound in the bottom of the ninth. Here's the 2–2 pitch...it's a high pop-up to center field...Aaron's coming under it...he's got his no-hitter, a perfect no-hitter! It's caught! Warren Spahn has just entered the Hall of Fame!"

I practiced until I had perfected every cadence, every dramatic pause, every cry of joy.

It was a natural progression from *Go Get 'Em, Braves* to other spoken-word albums. I listened to stand-up comedians and memorized their material, adding an array of voices to my repertoire. The laughs they earned from their nightclub audiences became my laughs. I was a hit.

It was downstairs, in that cavern, surrounded by all that joyful, dangerous, pulsating, riotous noise, that I first felt the rush of adrenaline, that liberating thrill that sent jolts of energy through my forehead and fingers and feet and yes even those forbidden private parts. I found a way to excite myself from head to toe, to escape from the boredom of life upstairs where there's homework and church and meatloaf and nothing much to do. The basement is where I first felt the rush of performing before an audience, even though the audience was only in my mind or on a prerecorded track.

And then there were the spy shows.

Fresh from devouring the latest episode of *The Man from U.N.C.L.E.* (the United Nations Command for Law Enforcement), I became Napoleon Solo, the handsome, elegant secret agent, skulking through the basement, dodging bullets behind the washing machine, shooting at enemy agents with a screwdriver or a wrench or anything that passed for a revolver. Once when I was home alone except for my mom cleaning the kitchen, I snuck upstairs, dressed myself in a shirt and tie and black pants, ran lukewarm water in the tub, and plunged fully clothed, submerging an enemy agent until he expired.

One afternoon, I was in full performance mode in the basement when I heard the upstairs door opening and the sound of my mother descending the steps. The stairs were hollow, so her normally petite tread sounded like someone three times her size. I stopped and threw myself into one of the cane chairs. I pulled a copy of *Boys' Life* out from under the cushion, turned to the Jokes page, and pretended to read; then, after letting about ten seconds elapse, I craned my neck ever so slightly, far enough to manage a glance at the stairs, just as Mom appeared. She was holding a basket of laundry, dressed as if she was about to go out for lunch: tan pumps, nylon stockings, carefully ironed housedress. June Cleaver had nothing on my mom.

When she got to the bottom of the stairs, she turned in the opposite direction, toward the laundry room, and quietly disappeared down the hallway.

Maybe she didn't see me.

Time to take the Show outside.

It was summer in Milwaukee. Cicadas whined away from sunrise to dusk. Cool breezes drifted through in the morning, giving way to muggy, sun-blanched afternoons. Clouds of mosquitoes and gnats relentlessly dive-bombed any human form brave enough to venture outside.

In the afternoons and early evenings when I thought no one was looking, I'd sneak out to the half-acre that stood behind our house, setting a breadbox-sized transistor radio at one end of the yard, and turning the dial to the station that broadcast the Braves' games.

The familiar jingle told me that the Braves were "on the air!"

Miller, Tareyton, and Clark

Take you out to the Park!

I loved the Braves. I scoured the sports section every day for news. I could recite their starting lineup and batting order. I memorized the names of every player on their roster, even the ones who seldom got in the game. I hoarded their baseball cards. I thought nothing of swapping half-a-dozen stars from other teams for just one missing Brave.

And on game days, I'd dress myself in my improvised Braves uniform, assembled from odds and ends, and I'd take the field, just one solitary kid embodying all the players. I took imaginary ground balls and shagged invisible outfield flies. I stood at the pitcher's mound, which in our yard was no more than a bald spot of grass no higher than the rest of the lawn, and I hurled screaming fastballs to home plate. Then I'd dash to home, squatting to take a toss from the ghostly pitcher. I was a solid utility player.

I loved pretending to run the bases, kicking up dirt as I'd execute a flawless hook slide, staining my uniform at the knees and elbows. A head-first slide was tough, because when I hit the grassy ground, I'd stop with a thud before I got to the base. But grass stains were OK too. Any evidence that I'd played hard was a badge of honor.

A tool shed that we called the "little garage" stood at one end of the yard. It held a lawn mower, various garden implements, and a circular basket stuffed with baseball gloves, bats, a catcher's mitt and mask, and a bright-red, waist-length life preserver that doubled ably as a catcher's chest protector. All the props I needed.

The best feature of the little garage was its location, just a few feet to the west of home plate. By setting up the dugout—a small wooden jungle gym draped with an old canvas covering—and leaning it up against the back wall of the garage, I was rendered invisible by prying eyes in the house, or so I thought. The dugout was an important staging area for my baseball enactments because it was from there that I conducted on-air interviews, invented heated contretemps between players, and performed inspirational pep talks from the manager before the team took the field.

My makeshift dugout was the first place where I ever felt like I was backstage, that secret place hidden away from the crowd. There were wonderful hiding places employed by adults that I had yet to discover: the tunnel under the bleachers in the arena from where the circus performers emerged, the sacristy adjacent to the altar at church, the dugouts at County Stadium where the Braves played, and, ultimately, the wings offstage. These safe havens were the hideouts where the performers huddled to prepare themselves before hurtling into the spotlight. It was where they gathered the courage to unveil themselves to the scrutiny of the audience.

When the real-life ballgame began, I'd turn up the volume on the radio and follow along with the play-by-play, acting out the game pitch by pitch. I'd follow the action for about an hour until my attention would flag or I'd get hungry, or I'd be interrupted by my brothers dashing out of the house without warning and I'd retreat to the privacy of my jungle gym dugout like a ball player enduring the annoyance of a rain delay. Throughout much of my reverie, my mom was mere yards away, bustling about in the kitchen, and often I wondered if she was watching me as she went about her housework. I was willing to risk embarrassment at being caught, because the world I was in fired my imagination and sent chills of excitement through my gawky, unathletic body. For a few minutes every day, I was Hank Aaron belting homers, or Warren Spahn mowing down hitters. Most importantly, I was not who I really was, an introverted, awkward kid. And my mom gave me the room to fill up my afternoons with pretending.

Eventually, she'd call me inside for lunch or a snack, and as I sat at the kitchen table, I'd utter secret thanks that she didn't make any jokes about what I was doing in the backyard. She was protective of my little secrets, and even then, I sensed there was something special about me in her heart because, in a family of six kids, I was the one who almost didn't make it.

(March 1958. Living room. Dishes clatter loudly offstage. A mix of ice and rain pelts the picture window directly across from the couch, where a four-year-old boy, JON, is moaning loudly. It feels as if monsters are eating away at his stomach, as JON presses his abdomen against the corners of a cushion to ease the pain. Footfalls rattle from upstairs, and in a moment another boy, the eldest brother by a few years, appears, his brows furrowed with worry. He calls in the direction of the kitchen.)

OLDEST BROTHER

Schatzie! He's crying again! I can hear him all the way upstairs!

SCHATZIE

(Calling)

I'm making him soup! He's hungry.

OLDER BROTHER

I think he needs to go to the doctor! He's all gray.

(The door to the outside swings open. AUNT BETTY hurries in, clutching a lit cigarette. AUNT BETTY leaves her bowling ball at the door and hurries to the couch.)

BETTY

Jon Bon, what's wrong?

JON

(Through tears and sweat)
It hurts! So bad!

(SCHATZIE, JON's grandmother, enters the living room. She's wiping her hands on a kitchen towel. Her eyes are wide with fear, and she looks frozen with panic.)

BETTY

Schatzie! We've got to get him to Dr. Conway! How long has he been like this?

OLDEST BROTHER

Since last night! He's really sick.

BETTY

(To SCHATZIE)
Bob and Marion would want him to see a doctor! They left us in charge! They're thousands of miles away, there's no phone service on a boat in the middle of the ocean! We've got to get him to a hospital!

(BETTY wraps JON in a blanket, scoops him into her arms, and hurries toward the door.)

SCHATZIE

(To OLDEST BROTHER)

Get his coat, it's cold out there!

BETTY

(To SCHATZIE)

There's no time for that. He'll be warm in my car. Terry can hold him in his arms, he's a big boy. Call the hotel where they're staying. Maybe they can cable them a message. What time is it in Hawaii?

(BETTY opens the door and rushes out. SCHATZIE and OLDER BROTHER exchange a look that frightens them both. Each knows what the other is thinking.)

SCHATZIE

He'll be all right. Don't you worry now.

(OLDER BROTHER turns on his heels and vaults up the stairs. SCHATZIE bustles into the kitchen.)

WHEN WE GOT TO the hospital, the admitting nurse wrapped my wrist in an ID bracelet with my name spelled wrong. I howled in protest. When she drew a blood sample, I fainted. When I came to, my clothes were damp with sweat and the top of my head was tingling. Betty held my hand as I was loaded on to a gurney and wheeled down the corridor to surgery.

When I woke up, Betty was sitting in a chair next to my bed. She gave me a book to read. My pain was gone. Time passed. And suddenly, I looked down to see my bed filling up with blood. It was coming out of my rectum, in torrents. A nurse rushed in, picked me up by the ankles and carried me off to surgery.

After two more operations, the bleeding finally stopped. Aunt Betty stayed at the hospital for three solid days. I was terrified of what was happening to me.

By the time my frantic parents finally made it home, I'd been given last rites by the hospital priest "just in case."

On a windswept, dreary Saint Patrick's Day, my parents rescued me from the scariest place I'd ever been and drove me home. My brothers struggled to avoid staring at their little brother, who was pale as an old T-shirt and ten pounds lighter than the fifty pounds I had weighed the week before. My dad nervously cracked a few jokes about renaming our house "Belly Acres on Ulcer Gulch" as my mom sat silently in the front seat, staring straight ahead, shielding me from the tears streaming down her face.

I went to bed for a month and my mom served me all the Jell-O and ice cream that I could eat, along with the special meals required by my ulcer diet. She gave me sponge baths, trying to distract me from staring at the two six-inch scars on my stomach and the sores formed by the intravenous tubes inserted in my ankles.

During the bleak month of my recovery, my mom became my protector. And once I emerged from bed and disappeared into my daydreams and make-believe, she gave me my solitude and the freedom to pretend without inhibition or fear of judgment. With her standing nearby yet out of sight, I could pretend and imagine all I wanted.

Chapter 3

OUT STANDING IN HIS FIELD

(1968. A hot, muggy summer day in Milwaukee. Almost dusk. JON, fourteen years old, has been visited by the puberty gods in the form of an overnight growth spurt and a reddish cluster of acne bursting across his cheeks. JON is standing in right field at St. Eugene's. This is not the safe haven of his imagination; it's a real-life baseball game. JON has been standing out there for hours. Nobody's hit a ball to him, which is the way he prefers it.)

I WAS HOPELESS AT this. I could *pretend* to be good because I watched games on TV. I could be the crafty righthander shaking off the catcher's signals, digging my left foot in the rubber, going into the windup, glancing at the runners at the corners, then firing a fastball down the middle. I could tug on my cap and wipe the sweat off my forehead just like a pro.

But once I got in a real game, my confidence wilted like week-old celery.

My knees were shaking with fear. My face flushed red, and not from the bright sun shining in my eyes. I dreaded the thought that the kid with the bat at home plate was going to hit one out where I was standing. I was the last kid chosen today, like always, and they stuck me out in right field where most of the time nobody hit the ball. But every so often somebody connected, and the ball hurtled toward me. Like last week. I heard the crack of the bat, I looked up, and there it was. As it approached, the air around me started to hum. The ground under me was shaking as the ball danced across my line of vision.

Hold still. Just catch it. It's not that hard to do.

But the ball shifted its path as it got close to me. I reached up over my head, forgetting to open my glove all the way. Not that it mattered. I missed it by a mile and the ball sailed over my head. I should have caught it. I could have caught it. But I panicked and stumbled a few feet to where the ball landed. I picked it up and launched a tremulous throw to the infield.

I blew it. Again.

Why do I do this to myself? So, I'm no good at baseball. Aren't there other things I can do?

I was good at some things. I was a good reader. I sang in the choir. I liked to listen to music. But when my "friends" and I got together, there was only one agenda: what game with a ball we were going to play.

I'd gotten one hit in my baseball career, a looping whimper that landed just past the first baseman's glove. I'd never had a forward pass thrown to me in the dozens of pickup football games I pretended to compete in. The only time I shot a basketball in a Catholic Conference game was a free throw, and I airballed it.

I hate this.

But I love to *pretend*. If only I could do *that* all the time.

The kid at the plate struck out. Finally, the inning was over. I ran back to the bench with relief. With any luck, I wouldn't have to bat. It was starting to get dark, so we'd be done soon.

It hadn't always been this bad. Just a few years ago when we were all three feet tall and uncoordinated, nobody cared about anything but running around and having fun. But then the stakes grew, the cream of athletic talent rose to the top, and the world divided into "jocks" and "feebs." Playground games got meaner, and competition became laced with confrontation. The friends with whom I'd been allies became tormentors. Maybe these guys had had tough skins all along, but by the time I'd discovered my shortcomings in the machismo department, it was too late for me to recover.

• ◆ •

At fourteen, I was old enough to be hired for my first job.

(1968. A dingy, stark, barely lit wooden shack on the grounds of an opulent country club. This is where the BOYS are waiting to be assigned to their "loop," the foursome of wealthy weekend golfers whose clubs they will tote around for three hours—that is, after a brief summer shower passes. Four boys are playing doubles ping-pong. Others hunch around a card table playing an impossibly convoluted card game called Sheepshead, razzing each other mercilessly with "table talk," trading insults like bubblegum cards. JON sits off by himself, reading a comic book and polishing off a Mountain Dew.)

("PB" and "JAY"—not their real names—swagger toward JON. They are among JON's oldest friends, having known him since kindergarten; but in recent times their relationship to JON has grown indifferent and often hostile. PB's body has retained the same compact, gracefully proportioned package it's always been. His mouth, newly fitted with wire braces, catches the light of the bare bulb hanging over his head. JAY, PB's current best friend, has more visible marks from puberty, including a face ravaged with acne and a ratty trace of a mustache, but he has rocketed up to a height of almost six feet while retaining his athletic prowess. He is the starting forward, the starting third baseman, the starring everything. He wears his status like a golden crown of entitlement.)

PB

(Sneering at JON, his ex-friend)
Look at the bookworm. Hey, Daly Bread, reading's for *fems*.

(JON buries his face in his Archie comic.)

PB

Hey. Daly Bread. I'm talking to you. What are you, some kind of pussy, sitting by yourself, reading a damn comic book? Good thing it's raining, I'd take you outside and kick your ass.

(PB's words cut through JON like jagged glass, but still he continues to read.)

PB

Hey, pussy, get up off your ass, can't you talk?

JAY

(Joining in the hazing)
Daly Bread! You gonna take that? Get up and fight, you pussy!

(JAY kicks at JON's feet, then grabs the edge of the bench JON is sitting on. JAY rocks the bench until JON has to stand up to keep from tumbling to the floor. JON reels toward the back door of the shack. Standing out in the rain would be preferable to taking more of this shit.)

(JON opens the door. PB slams it shut as JON pulls away his fingers at the last second.)

PB

What's the matter, pussy? You wanna run away and cry?

JON

Let me out!

PB

You gonna cry? Go ahead and cry!

(JON's heart is pounding. He's so angry and hurt that he loses control. JON grabs PB by the collar of his knit shirt, the kind that PB wears only on caddying days, so that he can fit in with the rich old men that he wants to impress on the golf course.)

PB

Go ahead! Hit me, pussy! I dare you!

(JON, gulping for air, pushes PB against the door. PB's eyes sparkle with surprise for just a moment before settling into the dull-eyed stare that perfectly matches the smug smirk on his lips.)

PB

You're not gonna do it! You're too scared! Afraid you're gonna hurt your little pussy hand! I oughta beat the shit out of you!

(JON releases his grip and pushes PB against the door. Now JON is crying. JON stumbles across the room and collapses onto a wooden bench. PB and JAY explode into more laughter and walk away, headed to the vending machine for more Pepsi.)

I COULDN'T STAND THE sound of him jeering at me. I jumped up and ran out the back door.

The rain stopped within a few minutes. The golfers emerged from their nineteenth hole a few drinks ahead of the game, and we were called in to work. The clouds cleared, the sun came out, a cool breeze lingered, and both storms—the cloudburst outside and the ruckus inside the caddy shack—had faded by lunchtime when I returned to the scene of my humiliation.

There was no sign of my tormentors. They probably went home after the first round of loops so they could spend the rest of the day pulling the wings off baby birds or beating up the neighborhood kids.

Good riddance. I'm done with them.

It was probably going to be another half hour before I got called out for my second round of the day, so I stepped out into the backyard of the shack. There was a big oak tree up a small incline, a nice spot for kids to gather and sit in the shade. I could hear peals of laughter coming from there. One guy was standing in front of the tree, and the other guys were seated around him, yukking it up and sometimes repeating what the standing kid was saying.

I recognized him. It was Bob, another guy I'd known since kindergarten. We'd been friends off and on over the years, but he lived on the other side of the Port Road, a good three miles from my house. I tended to hang around with the guys who lived closer to me, the jerks who I'd just sworn off for good. I'd always liked Bob. He was a jock too, but he wasn't obnoxious about it. And he liked to do other things. And apparently standing under a tree and telling jokes was one of them.

I got a few steps closer, and the words I was hearing started to sound familiar. I'd heard this before, but I just couldn't quite figure out where.

I stepped out of the backyard and got close enough to the tree that a couple of the kids turned to look at me. Bob kept talking, and suddenly I recognized what he was saying. It was one of the monologues I had perfected in my basement act.

I know this one!

I took the plunge and passed under the shade of the oak. Then I caught Bob's eye and started to speak, matching him word for word. After a couple of sentences, he called out, "You *know* this one?"

"Yeah! I know the whole first side," I beamed. I was halfway through learning the B side. I rifled through my brain for a good place to start. And then I was off, summoning all the characters, hitting all the punch lines spot on, even holding for laughs, which started coming from the audience under the tree. Bob was guffawing as loudly as anybody.

I was knocking it out of the park. And it wasn't baseball.

When I ran out of material, I stopped. And then I heard it.

Applause.

Just a handful of kids sitting in the shade of an oak tree, but they were smiling. And laughing. And clapping. For me.

"That's excellent. Man, I want to hear that whole album. You wanna come over tonight?" Bob offered.

I accepted. And just like that, I found a new crowd.

Rules for Actors, Rule #3: Make 'em laugh, and they'll like you.

After months of playing solo gigs in my basement and my backyard, I was out of hiding.

Chapter 4

WILD TIMES

IN THE SOCIAL JUNGLE that was the North Shore suburbs of Milwaukee, I shifted my allegiance to Bob and the other boys who occupied the unadorned blockhouses and cookie-cutter cottages along the fringes of the Port Road. They came from families with modest incomes and lots of kids. The boys were as unassuming as their houses, and I quickly fell in with them. They weren't that different from my previous tribe, the boys who lived closer to Lake Michigan; we organized ourselves into touch football games just like they had done, and we spent hours shooting baskets in Bob's backyard. But that sickening sense of peer pressure, of dreading being the last one picked, that was gone. Life with these guys was so much more fun.

We interjected two new elements into the mix: alcohol, and the thrilling fear of being caught. We wandered around the neighborhood after dark, ringing doorbells and dashing away like cockroaches exposed to the light. We stole six-packs of Schlitz from unattended garages. I snuck gin from my dad's liquor cabinet, squirreling away a little bit at a time so he wouldn't notice. After a few weeks, I'd have an eight-ounce Coke bottle filled to the brim with the stuff.

We needed someplace where we could hide away and puff away at my dad's Viceroys while breaking into the booze from his liquor cabinet. Then, we of the Port Road crowd suddenly got very interested in camping.

(Scene: just outside the Little Garage. MOM comes out the back door with a bag of garbage. JON has neglected to take out the trash, again.)

MOM

Where are you going, Jon?

JON

(Tying a large canvas bag to the back of his bike)
Over to Bob's.

MOM

You're spending the night again?

JON

We're gonna camp out.

MOM

It's going to get down into the forties tonight. Won't you be cold?

JON

(Being careful not to jiggle the glass bottle wrapped up in the canvas)
We'll bundle up. See you tomorrow!

(Exit, pedaling away with the EZ Way Four-Man Tent, vodka, and cigarettes)

THEN, THERE WAS THE night that the stakes got as high as we were.

We were crowded into the tent: Bob; me; Bob's next-door neighbor Pete, a shy kid with thick glasses, a surprisingly deep baritone, and a caustically dry wit; and Freddie, a kid down the street with a high-pitched laugh and the demeanor of a manic chipmunk.

We'd pedaled our bikes to the 7-Eleven just after nightfall, pooling our pennies to buy a quart of Pirate's Gold orange juice. We'd cycled home on Port Road, flying along on the gravel shoulder and avoiding being hit by the cars speeding by. Then we'd bundled into the safety of the tent, and the party began, in hushed tones so Bob's parents, in the house less than twenty yards away, couldn't hear us.

We mixed ourselves ridiculously strong screwdrivers and drank until our heads were spinning and every joke we told was the funniest damn thing we'd ever heard. The tent filled up with smoke. We munched on Fritos and saltines.

Fortified with food and drink, we brainstormed plans for the rest of the evening.

I spoke up first. "Let's go over to Sherry Maynard's house and bang on the windows."

Maybe I'll see her in her nightgown, who knows?

"Let's ride our bikes through the cemetery!" Bob said, looking around for approbation.

Freddie chirped, "Let's sneak over to the swimming pool on Mohawk Road and go skinny-dipping."

"Too cold," I said. "My mom says it's gonna get down to 40."

But Freddie was undeterred. He fired back with the best idea of the night.

"Let's run around the block naked!"

We all stage-whispered our approval, and I was the first to pull off my shirt and pants and peel off my underwear, keeping my shoes on so I could run on the asphalt. Pete, Bob, and Freddie quickly followed, and all four of us streaked down the street.

"Let's go wave at the cars on the highway," Bob said.

We cut through backyards and side streets until we got to the interstate. My hands were numb from the cold. My nose was running. But alcohol and adrenaline were keeping the rest of me warm.

We scaled the chain-link fence, miraculously sparing any damage to our budding sexual organs. The icy steel pressed against my thighs, and I jumped to the ground below.

Traffic was light tonight, and we hid in the bushes, giggling, out of breath, tickled pink with our daring. I started to shiver.

Then a car appeared in the distance.

Here we go. Do I have the balls to do this?

Yes.

I leaped out of the bushes, lurched to the edge of the road, and started waving. Pete, Bob, and Freddie were right next to me. We started yelling. My head was spinning.

It was a big old Buick. Its lights shifted to high beams. The car slowed down. The tires crunched on the gravel. He was stopping!

We sprinted toward the fence and scaled it. When I got to the top, I cupped my scrotum in my hands before leaping to the grass below.

We cut through yards, skittered down driveways, descended into ditches. Whoever had stopped for us couldn't possibly reach us, because their nearest exit ramp was a mile away.

Within the first block, we'd separated. It was every kid for himself. Me and Freddie skipped through a side yard and ended up in the back of a house where all the lights were off. We were both running out of steam, so we took a second to catch our breaths, leaning up against the back wall of the house. In a moment we heard a voice booming out from the other side of the bedroom window:

"Hey! Who izzat? What the hell you doin' out there?"

Freddie was the first to bolt. I pushed to keep up with him, guided by the glow of his little white butt cheeks in the moonlight. My numbed dick was bobbing and slapping against my crotch. I was sweating a ton, but it evaporated as soon as I felt it run down my spine. I caught up to Freddie and I could smell the gin on his breath and the acrid scent of his body.

I finally reached his side. We looked at each other and laughed, our giggles turning to breathy guffaws as we struggled to keep up the pace of our sprinting. We were getting away with it. We were going to be all right.

After that night, Freddie and I became each other's favorite sleepover pals. He had several younger brothers and sisters, all of whom shared his impish sense of humor. With their pug noses, square jaws, aquamarine eyes, and unruly mops of straw-colored hair, they were a clown troupe to themselves. Freddie and I developed a repertoire of funny voices and improvisational nonsense that had us entertained for hours. And behind it all was the memory of that Rabelaisian night of danger that we shared, sprinting through the neighborhood.

(Two weeks later. Late afternoon of a sweltering day in August. JON's bedroom. He is sitting on the bed with FREDDIE, playing a cutthroat card game of War. FREDDIE is having an incredible string of good luck. JON is down to his last card, and FREDDIE draws a queen. JON is wiped out. FREDDIE twists his face into a mock grimace, squints at JON from behind narrowed eyes, and barks in his best tough-guy voice.)

FREDDIE
That's it, Mister. Off with your shirt.

(JON complies, tossing his T-shirt in FREDDIE'S face. Freddie stands up, walks over to the bedroom door, and locks it.)

FREDDIE
Now your PANTS!

(JON feels a rush of adrenaline to his sternum, then kicks off his sneakers and pulls his pants down around his ankles. His arms are shaking. JON flings his pants as hard as he can into FREDDIE's outstretched arms.)

FREDDIE
Now your JOCKEYS!

(JON steps out of his underwear and is standing naked in front of his best friend. There is a gawky pause. It's his turn to give the orders, and JON knows it. FREDDIE waits, his cheeks flushed bright red. JON stares him down and imitates his tight-jawed growl.)

JON

Your *SHIRT.*

(FREDDIE laughs, then complies.)

JON

Now your PANTS, Mister.

(FREDDIE's guffaws turn to nervous giggles as he pulls off his pants.)

JON

And now the rest…

(FREDDIE strips off his underwear. FREDDIE and JON stand facing each other, tittering like hyenas. Their shallow breaths come in gulps. Goose pimples pop up on the insides of their arms. The scent of adolescent male nakedness fills the stuffy air. Suddenly FREDDIE and JON grab on to each other, wrestling lamely until they land in a heap on the bed. FREDDIE and JON pull the covers over their heads and lock together, cackling in hushed gasps as they ball their legs up in a tangle, their knees knocking as they grind their quivering bodies together.)

(There's a knock on the bedroom door. It's MOM. She calls from the hallway.)

MOM

"Oh, boys…Freddie's parents are here to take him home."

(FREDDIE and JON careen out of the bed as if they've touched a live wire. The scene ends prematurely, or maybe just in the nick of time.)

FREDDIE WAS BACK IN his clothes as fast as he shed them. I hopped around idiotically, trying to jump into my pants.

He galloped down the stairs to the front door, me following sheepishly. Freddie scurried out the door like a mobster evading reporters and folded himself into the backseat of the station wagon, which was swaying crazily to the rhythm of the other kids jostling for who gets to sit next to their big brother. Freddie stole a look to me, a mischievous sparkle in his eyes. Their car pulsed away, with me left standing stupidly on the flagstone porch, my insteps straining to find their balance so the rest of my body could catch on and stop wobbling.

A voice in my head was chattering away like the crows cawing in the trees. I darted up the stairs and hurled myself on my bed. I had to think.

We were naked. No kissing. No touching dicks. No hugging. Just a lot of scuffling and giggling.

Would I rather do all that with Sherry Maynard? Definitely. Not that I'd ever have the nerve to try.

So why can I do it with Freddie?

You didn't do anything. You were just messing around. You just happened to be naked.

I'd never really thought about it before. I'd seen foldout pinups of naked girls. And then there had been the day that a kid in my neighborhood had shown me pictures from a nudist magazine that he'd found hidden in a drawer in his dad's desk. *Everybody* was naked.

I'm almost sure that I like girls.

I put my hand down my pants and started rubbing. I thought about Sherry Maynard.

I sighed with relief.

Yeah. I like girls.

Chapter 5

MY MOTHER MADE ME DO IT

ONE OF THE GOOD things about going to an all-boys high school is that they import girls from other schools to act in the plays put on by the drama club. At age fourteen and starting my freshman year, I had never been in a play, but the possibility of girls brightening up the scene made me seriously consider auditioning.

The Prep Players had been producing plays since the opening of the high school in 1924. My dad had won the Director's Medal for Acting in 1935 for his performance as Polonius in *Hamlet*. His name was inscribed in gold on a brass plate just outside the auditorium.

In recent years, Father McIntyre, a short, dapper, bespectacled chain smoker of Lark nonfiltered cigarettes, had become the Players' director and had produced musicals to great acclaim. My freshman year was *West Side Story*.

In my English class that year, we'd studied *The Merchant of Venice*, the first Shakespeare play I'd ever read. I didn't understand most of it, but when Mr. Horner made me get up in class and read a scene where I played Shylock, I was really surprised at how much sense it made. I raised my voice, I pounded the lectern, I felt angry and resentful and a little unleashed, and it all seemed to come from the words on the page. This was cool. It nearly gave me the courage to audition for *West Side Story*, but when I got to the heavy wooden door of the auditorium and saw my dad's name on the brass plate, I lost my nerve.

I tried again the following year when the Players did *Camelot*. If you got in, you'd get to wear doublet and tights and a cape, and you could even grow your hair over your collar. But you had to try out by singing a song. I could do that in my basement just fine, all by myself. But get up on the stage and do it in front of people? No way. I was having a hard enough time figuring out how I fit in to this school with a thousand other guys. I wasn't about to make an idiot of myself. So once again I chickened out.

Rules for Actors, Rule #4: If you don't try out, you won't get a part.

• ◆ •

I SPENT MY SOPHOMORE year dragging my sorry ass around the gloomy hallways. I struggled through biology and geometry and barely managed a high C average. I felt morose and invisible.

One afternoon as I sulked at the kitchen table, my mom placed a newspaper at my side when she served me lunch. As I munched away on my bologna sandwich and potato chips, she pointed to the article at the bottom of the page.

"Have you seen this?" she asked.

"What is it?" I answered, not really caring to hear the answer.

"It's a play. Maybe you'd like to be in a play?"

It was a notice for an audition at the local children's theater.

Yuck. What makes her think I'd want to do this? "Walk The Plank!" (?) Sounds stupid.

"Why don't you think about it?" she suggested. "Maybe you'd like it." She took my empty plate to the sink and left me alone with the paper.

A week later, she was driving me down to the Lutheran church for the tryout. I did it to get her off my back.

When I got out of the car, Mom smiled at me and said, "Good luck!"

I gave her a sullen glare, lurched out of the front seat, slammed the door, and climbed the stairs with as much attitude as I could summon.

I pulled open the big wooden door to the sanctuary and stepped into the breezeway as the door sucked shut with a clanking slam. Penciled-in arrows on a crumpled piece of paper directed me to descend squeaky wooden steps into the basement.

There was an ancient white-haired lady, wearing a cloth cape and silver turban, sitting behind a card table. She handed me a piece of paper and told me to write down my name and phone number. Then she gave me a small paperback book with a bookmark stuck in it.

"You'll be reading for 'Second Mate.' He's a young seafarer, very proud and strong."

Why am I doing this? And why don't I get to read FIRST Mate?

"You'll be reading with Maggie. She's the heroine of the story. Go on, go on in…"

I walked into a room with white walls, a low ceiling, and fluorescent lights. There were folding chairs scattered around the room. Pipes ran along the ceiling.

A girl holding a script like mine looked up. She had long golden hair that flowed halfway down her back. In the middle of winter, her skin was tan, and she looked like she was blushing. Her eyes were bright blue. She smiled, and I could see her white teeth. As I got closer to her, I could smell perfume.

"Hi," she said in a quiet little voice. "My name is Maggie."

Oh please let me get this.

Chapter 6

THE PLAY'S
THE THING

(The curtain opens on GWENDOLYN, the beautiful daughter of the Earl of Tramplemain. She has been taken prisoner by a band of PIRATES on her way back home to the mainland. Dressed in a pink pinafore dress, her long fair hair is floating in waves and pooling around her dainty shoulders. GWENDOLYN is seated on a wooden ship's beam that looks suspiciously like a stool covered in papier-mâché. She is holding a petite doll swathed in pink crinoline, and she consoles herself with a song taught to her by her mother, the Countess of Tramplemain.)

GWENDOLYN
(Singing)
A countess's child will not complain
When weather turns to storm and rain....

(Her song is interrupted by the entrance of SECOND MATE, meant to be coming from a great distance but, in reality, only from the janitor's closet two feet offstage. He is tall and ridiculously skinny and he is wearing a suede vest and velour pants cut off at his bony knees. He is slathered from head to toe in red greasepaint the color

of a county park picnic table, the stain being made to suggest a life spent at sea under a raging sun. His head is covered by a black wig that looks like it's made from yarn, adorned with pigtails and topped with a leather band. He is a walking cliché, an adult's vision of a child's pirate fantasy.)

(Upon his entrance, SECOND MATE turns his gaze in the direction of the janitor's closet and extends his naked arm to indicate that he and GWENDOLYN are about to be joined onstage by other characters. SECOND MATE releases a few labored breaths to indicate that he has run a great distance. Then he looks to GWENDOLYN, pretending not to notice her beautifully tanned shoulders, her lustrous yellow hair, and the seductive scent of the Intimate perfume she must have splashed on her neck and arms just before curtain. He takes a deep breath and declaims the first line he has ever delivered on any stage.)

SECOND MATE

Aye, aye, Mistress! Afore you they are here!

(Enter BOBTAIL JACK, the Pirate Captain, played by a longtime veteran of the community theater. BOBTAIL JACK is wearing an ill-fitting spotted vest over his bare torso, his pendulous belly exposed, much to his chagrin. He is accompanied by FIRST MATE, who for some unknown reason has ten more lines than SECOND MATE.)

BOBTAIL JACK

(Pounding the stage with his walking stick to indicate that he's in charge here, and adjusting his eyepatch, which tends to slip down toward his cheek, a gesture he will repeat with increased irritation throughout the afternoon.)

AVAST AND ALACK, DAUGHTER OF MY ENEMY, THE LAND-GRUBBING TRAMPLEMAIN. YOU ARE NOW IN THE HOLD OF BOBTAIL JACK!

FIRST MATE
AYE, AYE, BOBTAIL JACK!

(SECOND MATE consoles himself that he shouldn't be all that disappointed that FIRST MATE has more lines, as he spends most of the time simply repeating what BOBTAIL JACK says, for emphasis.)

GWENDOLYN
I fear you not, pirate! I am the daughter of a mighty emperor.

BOBTAIL JACK
(Puffing up his chest in a vain attempt to hide the rolls in his stomach)
You are my prisoner until your father produces the ransom I demand.

FIRST MATE
Aye, Aye! The ransom we demand!

GWENDOLYN
And what *is* your demand?

BOBTAIL JACK
Gold doubloons and pieces of eight!

FIRST MATE
(Repeating again, ho hum)
Aye, aye! Pieces of eight!

SECOND MATE
(Rearing up for his best lines of the whole afternoon; it's all downhill from here.)
We demand no less from the thieving villain of Tramplemain!!

GWENDOLYN
My father is not a villain! You are the villains!

SECOND MATE

(Seizing the stage with all the authority that a fifteen-year-old can muster)

By all that is just and proper, WE ARE IN THE RIGHT!!

WE PRESENTED THIS DRIVEL in at least two locations every weekend for three months, sometimes doing as many as three performances in a day. We played churches, grade schools, recreation centers, and Kiwanis Club basements, and sometimes even real theaters with soft plushy seating that squeaked and rattled as our restless audience shifted and squirmed, rightfully bored with the pompous, stilted dialogue and story.

As bad as it was, my mom was right: I *did* like it. She came to the first performance, and when I got in the car with her afterward, she looked relieved. She was just happy to see me involved with something to get me out of my shell. And I was happy because I was going to spend the next two months of weekends being with Maggie.

(Scene: The backseat of JON's mother's Ford Torino sedan. It's cold outside, but the roads are dry. MAGGIE and JON are sitting close to each other as the Torino passes along fields of fallow prairie. The trees are bare. The sky is murky with thick clouds. The parkas they are wearing are providing MAGGIE and JON with a snug boundary, intimacy hinted at but carefully controlled.)

JON

What was the first play you were ever in?

MAGGIE

The Sound of Music. I was six.

JON

I saw *The Sound of Music* when I was six. It was the first play I ever saw.

MAGGIE

Mine was in Chicago. It was a tour. We went to St. Louis, and Cincinnati, all kinds of places.

JON

You did *The Sound of Music* in Chicago? That's where I saw it!

(JON can't see it, but his mother is grinning from the front seat.)

MAGGIE

Then I guess you saw me....

(JON breathes through his nose, and the scent of Intimate perfume fills his head. MAGGIE's shoulder is lightly pressed against his in the crowded back seat. JON makes no attempt to move away.)

JON

Are you from Milwaukee?

MAGGIE

Michigan. Benton Harbor. We moved here last year. My mom got married again after my dad died, and we all moved here. All my friends are back in Benton Harbor. My mom said I should be in a play so I can meet new people....

(JON has never known anyone whose father died. His heart flutters with an empathy he's never felt in his whole life. He wants desperately to put his arm around her.)

MAGGIE

But I've been to Milwaukee before. I was in *The King and I* when I was ten.

JON

In Washington Park? With Yul Brynner? I saw that one too!

(JON turns to face her. His parka is bunching up against his neck, as the zipper scrapes against his throat. He wishes he could take his coat off; he's more than warm enough. MAGGIE is smiling at him. The gloss on her cheeks: Is it from the cold air, or is it makeup? Whatever it is, it's stunning. Her teeth are two straight lines of creamy ivory. JON aches to kiss her. He's never kissed a girl. This would be a good time to start. They are facing forward in the seat, letting the silence draw them even closer together. Out of the corner of his eye, JON can see MAGGIE's hand on her lap. He reaches out to hold it, and she lets him do it. The rest of the drive passes in tender bliss.)

AFTER TWO MONTHS HAD passed and we were finished with the play, Maggie and I had become inseparable. We spent the summer as fixtures in each other's living rooms, watching television until our parents went to bed and then indulging in fervent petting: chaste kisses for the first half hour and then advancing to open-mouthed mashing, breathing through our noses before coming up for air. One night I reached inside Maggie's blouse, and she let me touch her breast. That was the same night that we sat on her front porch, unable to tear ourselves away from each other, composing our future wedding invitations and with Maggie filling page after page of her pink stationery with her married name. That summer it seemed as if there was a full moon every night, or that I was in the middle of one long, starry night that I hoped would never end.

In the fall, I took her to our homecoming dance, and she invited me to be on her prom court. She got the leading role in her high school's spring play, and suddenly I developed the nerve to try out for my school's musical. I got in. I wanted to keep up with Maggie. Being in plays, even separate ones, kept us connected. And the more plays I was in, the more confident I got.

I began writing and performing sketches for assemblies and pep rallies. I joined the cheerleading squad. I ran for president of the student council and lost. Some of my friends tried to put me down for being on an "ego trip" by doing all this public performing, but I didn't care. I'd found my way to survive high school.

In my senior year, I auditioned for the spring musical, *Oliver*. I'd seen the movie, and I couldn't imagine myself in any of the roles. I wasn't mean enough to play Bill Sikes. I thought Mr. Brownlow was kind of boring. But I auditioned for Fagin, the devious, charming old ringleader of a gang of youthful pickpockets. I had a whole bunch of songs to sing. I had to speak in a British accent. It was a *leading role*.

And I got it.

I threw myself into the part, and I was surprised how it came almost naturally to me, even though Fagin exceeded me in age by at least three decades. The songs were in a key I could reach, the accent was easy to find, and the scenes were so much fun to do.

When I put on my costume the day of dress rehearsals, I didn't recognize myself. I wore a stringy shoulder-length wig, I built a mustache out of crepe hair, and my skinny teenaged body was thoroughly disguised by a cloth coat that stretched all the way to my calves, worn over corduroy knickers, dirty gray leggings, and black slippers with bows attached at the instep. I squeezed the floppy black hat over my wig, took a last look at myself in the mirror, and then climbed the circular stairs to the stage.

The next three hours were the most fun I'd had in my life. The words poured out of me. I sang as if this was the most natural thing for me to do, and everybody else on stage was playing along with me. It was what I'd always wanted sports to be, only better.

Father McIntyre sat us down for a note session after it was all over. His legal pad was filled with notes. He lit up a Lark and pummeled us with reminders to speak louder, or to pick up our cues, or to make sure we were standing in range of the standing mikes spaced around the stage.

When it was all over, I stood up and pushed the wooden seat, now damp with my sweat, back to its upright position. I was negotiating the downhill glide from the orchestra seats to the pit that led to the dressing rooms when Father McIntyre stopped me.

"Mister Daly, I don't want you to get a big head about this."

To be sure, I was pretty taken with myself. I was learning about the powerful adrenaline that shoots through your veins after you've spent a night acting your heart out. My face and neck pulsed wildly, and my clothes were sticky with sweat. I tried to wipe the silly grin on my face, but it lingered. I was on such a high.

Father McIntyre looked me straight in the eye. He wasn't finished.

"All I want to say is that you might want to think about doing this for a living. You're really quite exceptional."

I couldn't think of anything to say. I'd never received such a compliment. About anything I'd ever done.

"Now go home and get some sleep. You've got to do it again tomorrow."

I eased my way down the wooden steps to the tunnel underneath the stage.

I changed into my street clothes and walked outside. As I stood in the parking lot waiting for my mom to pick me up and drive me home, I heard myself say to the night sky, "That's it. I know what I'm going to be."

Chapter 7

DAD

(1972. Kitchen table. Just past dusk. MOM is just seating herself at the table opposite DAD. Plates of meatloaf, mashed potatoes, and green beans are being passed. There is a moment of quiet. JON fixes his gaze on his dinner but senses that DAD's focus is on JON's hair. DAD adjusts his glasses and launches into a familiar observation, as the other boys sigh and relax, pleased to be released from the tonsorial Hot Seat for once. The younger girl in the family is exempt. The older girl is away at college.)

DAD

Hey, Schmitt, that hair is getting long.

JON

I just got it cut.

DAD

You must be mistaken.

When were you last at the barber shop?

JON

I don't know, I don't remember every haircut. There are so many of them.

DAD

Well, you'd better take care of it soon as possible. You're starting to look like a girl—

JON

I like the way it looks.

DAD

—or a Beatle. Go on Monday.

JON

The barber shops are closed on Monday.

DAD

Nonsense. I get my haircut at the club every other Monday.

JON

Barber shops don't have the same hours. They close on Mondays.

DAD

(Turning to MOM)
Marion, is that true?

MOM

They're closed on Mondays.

DAD

What about that one in Whitefish Bay?

MOM

Closed.

DAD

There's that one next to the grocery store.

MOM

> Closed, Bob.

DAD

> I never heard of such a thing.

MY FAILINGS WERE THE only thing my dad and I ever seemed to talk about. My hair was too long. I didn't sit up straight. I left my stuff scattered all over the house. I didn't appreciate the comfortable life he provided. But I had little in common with the authoritarian workaholic who glared at me from across the dinner table.

I carried resentment on my shoulders like an overstuffed knapsack. I hadn't the slightest idea how to relate to him. And I didn't care enough to find out.

Over the years, I'd heard the stories of him growing up during the Depression, of being the oldest of five kids, of enlisting in the army and becoming a navigator in World War II. My mom loved to tell the tale of how he showed up on her doorstep one day, intent on keeping their date despite having a raging fever and being exhausted from his eighteen-hour days as a law student and part-time employee at Max Goldberg's furniture store, and how he passed out when she opened the door, falling into her arms and spilling his sprig of flowers all over the front stoop.

He was a hard worker and very responsible. Yeah, I got that. But I also smelled the alcohol on his breath every night, and every so often his dinnertime pontifications were delivered with slightly slurred speech and repetitions of phrases that made me want to leap up from the table and escape.

I got used to the smell of Scotch on him. It was as omnipresent as his aftershave. He never missed work, he avoided scenes, and I hardly ever saw him sway or stumble. But there was the one summer afternoon at a family party when I saw him tip over in a wooden chair, the soles of his shoes dangling in the air. I heard people laughing. I didn't think it was funny. What if he was hurt?

His Scotch came in a green bottle with Scottie dogs on the label. When I was nine, I sat in my dad's Cadillac, watching the snow flurries dance in the headlights of the car and spying the man at the counter of the little shop off the highway where we'd stopped. As Dad stood at the counter, the little man with the red goatee put each bottle in a cardboard sleeve and wrapped the whole thing in a brown paper bag. I couldn't wait to get home. I snagged one of the boxes before he threw them in the trash. Its rectangular shape looked to me just like a miniature version of a coffin.

I took the box up to my room, along with a rectangular piece of cardboard cribbed from Dad's dry-cleaned shirts. I drew a picture on the cardboard of a man in a suit, his eyes closed, his arms laid upon his chest; I cut out the figure carefully with my scissors and placed the cardboard corpse in the box. Then I wrapped the box in a small American flag and stole out to the bushes behind our house where I dug a hole and consigned his paper remains to the final resting place. I performed this ritual—except for the flag; I only had the one—every week during the winter of 1963, after I'd spent hours in front of the TV watching the funeral services for JFK.

Eventually, I tired of the backyard burials, but I kept collecting the liquor boxes. Dad was going through the Scotch with a quickening pace, and I couldn't have kept up with him even if I'd wanted to. Soon I had a stack of boxes piled up on the inside wall of my closet. I thought I'd keep them for storing baseball cards, but shoeboxes were much better.

My mom asked me why I was keeping all these empty boxes. "They're the boxes that Dad's bottles come in," I told her. She looked annoyed as she hauled them away, but maybe she was fretting about how many boxes there were.

Outside of profiting from Dad's Scotch consumption, I had precious little to tie us together. Dad had no hobbies to share with me. He didn't fish, he didn't play golf or go on bike rides or play catch in the backyard. He didn't collect stamps or read books to me at night. He didn't like to listen to music except as background to conversation among adults. Bach concertos, jazz collections, Big Band Swing—to him, all of it was just a lot of showing off.

But every now and then he would call me into the living room and pronounce, "It's time for a horse race." He'd reach into the drawer of the end table that sat next to his easy chair, and he'd pull out a sheet of Magic-Race horse-racing flash paper. With a slightly trembling hand, he'd apply the flaming end of his Viceroy cigarette to the black flag printed at one end of the paper. Slowly the flame would spread, and then split into five distinct lines, each line corresponding to a horse at the starting gate. As he held the flash paper ten inches off the floor, the "race" would begin. He provided the commentary, speaking in the trumpet-like cadences of the racetrack announcer:

"Aaaand they're off! It's War Admiral in the lead, The Chief coming up on the outside, it's Seabiscuit…Seabiscuit…and now here comes Night Mare on the inside, she's closing in…Seabiscuit gaining ground, War Admiral falling behind…and it's Seabiscuit! Seabiscuit by a nose! Listen to this crowd!"

I could see an actor lurking deep in his distant, preoccupied soul. The evidence of it dotted the walls of our den in the form of photos of him as a member of the Prep Players. Dad as the lead gumshoe in a detective story, Dad as the romantic lead in a drawing-room comedy, Dad as Polonius.

When I was nine, our parish church produced a variety show of songs and sketches, many of which were inspired by nostalgia for a bygone time when men wore cutaways, striped trousers and spats, and women promenaded in long dresses and high-button shoes. Men tipped their top hats to the ladies, and the ladies smiled like ingenues, their laced bonnets sparkling in the stage lights. A nod to a period that had ceased to exist long before their own wartime youth, but it was all very grand and proper. It was as if their revels were inspired by episodes of *The Lawrence Welk Show*, which was all the rage at the time. I groaned outwardly when my parents turned on that program, rolling my eyes at the incorrigible hokeyness of it all.

But that night in the church hall, seeing it live and up close, was entirely different, especially when my dad took center stage, resplendent in a midnight-blue suit with wide pinstripes, a straw hat tipped at a jaunty angle on his head, leaning on his cane and singing to a chorus of somewhat dowdy chorines, all of them cooing and ogling him as if he were Rudy

Vallée. It was a side of my dad that he otherwise hid away like a box of old clothes in the attic. And he was *good*. He sang in a bright, pleasing baritone. He smiled like he hadn't a care in the world. And I beamed right along with him. On that magical night in 1963, I saw my dad sing and dance.

(1972. Spring. JON's bedroom. JON is sitting on the bed in his pajamas, trying to calm down after the opening night of Oliver. *Headphones on, he is listening to his new obsession, Wendy Carlos's* Switched-On Bach. *He doesn't hear the soft tap, and in a moment the door opens a crack. DAD is standing there in his robe and slippers, holding a Viceroy between his index and middle fingers. It's burning down to the filter. He glances around the room. He hasn't spent any time in here for years. JON takes off his headphones. There is a pause.)*

DAD
You did a good job tonight.

JON
Thanks.

DAD
Time for you to fold up. It's almost midnight. See how fast you can get to sleep.

JON
I will, Dad.

DAD
Goodnight.

JON
Goodnight.

(DAD closes the door and is gone.)

I SAT AT THE edge of the bed, and I felt a ripple of warmth from deep in my chest.

He'd said, "You did a good job."

I'd wanted to say something to him in return. I wanted to ask him about *Hamlet* all those years ago. I wanted him to sit down and talk to me about acting in plays. I wanted to tell him that I'd decided what I wanted to do with my life. I was going to go to college and major in theater. Then I was going to be an actor.

Instead, I was staring at a closed door, as the lightness in my heart faded into a loneliness that settled over me like a snow cloud in February.

I crawled into bed, turned off the lamp, and burrowed under the covers. My thoughts raced, my heart longing for something that I couldn't quite define, but which I was missing.

I couldn't fall asleep just yet. I had an idea, and by the time I finally drifted off, I had a plan.

Chapter 8

VOLPONE

I THOUGHT IT WAS brilliant in its simplicity. I was going to talk my dad into taking me to see a play at the Rep.

The Milwaukee Repertory Theater was founded in 1954, the same year that I was born. In 1966, when I was in sixth grade, the Rep installed a resident acting company, and by the time I was in high school, the company had risen in prestige to the point that it was considered one of the finest ensembles in the United States. Their repertoire was eclectic: Shakespeare, Chekhov, American realism, European farce, and experimental plays. I idolized the actors; they were the role models for my future. I wanted to be them when I grew up.

School was where I'd get the training that I'd need. I had it all figured out. But my dad would be paying the bills, so I had to break it to him that I didn't want to major in prelaw or accounting or business administration. It was hard for me to talk with my dad about anything, let alone something as serious as my future.

So, I'd go with him to the Rep, a place he'd never been, to see one of their lavish productions. Next up was a seventeenth-century English comedy called *Volpone*. This was perfect. Surely when he beheld the brilliant acting, the gorgeous sets, the lights, the costumes, then he'd understand my excitement, open his checkbook, and ask me where I wanted to go to school. I was hopeful that seeing all these wonderful actors would reawaken the actor in him, and that my ambition would become his for me. And maybe, at the same time, we could find something that might connect us to each other. Maybe we could find something to talk about besides the length of my hair.

I asked my dad if he'd take me to see it, and lo and behold, he said yes. We hadn't done anything together, just him and me, in…well…*ever*.

On the night of the play, I dressed up in a suitcoat and tie and Dad drove me downtown in his current company car, a white Buick Electra, a tugboat in which I normally hated to be seen. I usually insisted that Dad drop me off a block away from my destination so that my friends wouldn't see me pull up, like Richie Rich being dropped off by his chauffeur.

But tonight was different. I was going to *the theatuh*.

I strode down the center aisle, gazing around at all the well-dressed patrons. I fit right in. I settled into the plush velvet seat and tried not to gawk at the magnificent set. The stage floor was painted to look like priceless marble. The walls were studded with gold sconces. The whole place looked like the Palace of Versailles. And the music, played by a full orchestra (on tape), filled the acoustically perfect space.

I glanced at my dad. He was paging through the program, reading all the advertisements for furs, luxury cars, and investment brokers.

The lights dimmed. I sat in the dark with my heart fluttering. I had stopped breathing for a moment, just waiting to be transported to this glamorous, enchanting world.

The scene lights came up. Actors burst onto the stage. They were alive with plots and cons and delicious asides to us, the audience. Lustful, profane sycophants, speaking in verse, shaming themselves while flattering the con man who drinks in all the flattery and seduction like the charming, greasy rogue that he is. It was wicked, it was hilarious, and it was flawlessly performed. When the lights came up for intermission, I turned to my dad, restraining myself from saying what I felt: "Isn't this GREAT?"

But Dad spoke first. "Well, I don't much care for this."

My words piled up in the back of my throat like cars stuck in a traffic jam. Had we been watching the same play? I hadn't felt this excited since Bart Starr quarterback sneaked his way through the Dallas Cowboys defensive line in the '67 Super Bowl. This was better. My dad's indifference poked me in the chest and opened a hole in my lungs.

"You don't like it?" I invited, stifling my impulse to scream.

He issued his critique in one phrase: "Nothing *happened*."

What the hell are you talking about? The plot is clearly presented, the actors are fantastic, there's more action than in a high-speed car chase, and you say NOTHING HAPPENED?

Those words stayed trapped inside me. Instead, I said, "Oh. That's too bad."

He stood up. "I'll be in the lobby. If you want to watch the second act, I'll wait for you."

And he left. Deserted me in the middle of our night together.

I stung with humiliation and disappointment. And my face burned with embarrassment that I was suddenly sitting next to the only empty chair in the whole orchestra section. The connection I had hoped to kindle sputtered into the night.

I'm not going to let him spoil this for me.

The stage lights came up for the second act, and I forgot all about it. And him. The play took me over.

Volpone didn't let me down. The second act was even more spectacular than the first, and when the curtain call came, I clapped so hard my hands ached. The muscles in my jaw hurt from smiling. I belonged in this room, with these people, with all this spectacle. I could have stayed in my seat and watched it all over again.

I ascended the carpeted stairs with the rest of the audience, working my way into the lobby, where the walls were covered with displays from recent productions. I wanted to take them all in, gazing at the color photographs of the resident acting company, but I had to find my dad. Even though our time spent together had been a dismal failure, he was my ride home.

I found him sitting on a bench closest to the exit, his coat carefully folded over his lap, fedora planted on his head. Before I got within six feet of him, I could smell the Scotch. He'd obviously spent the second act in the bar across the street.

He stood up, a little unsteady, and we walked in silence to the car several blocks away.

"Do you want me to drive?" I asked.

"Of course not," he said. "You can close your eyes if you want. You must be tired."

We rode in silence. As the minutes passed, my insides bubbled with anger. At him. And at myself, for being such an idiot.

He never asked me why I loved the play so much. He never asked me anything about it.

Over the next few months, I made a few more feeble attempts to connect with him. I tried using the big bands as my way in, the music he must have listened to when he was my age. I couldn't get enough Glenn Miller and Benny Goodman. I crashed his post-dinner reading time one night, grabbing one of his albums out from under the dusty record rack, putting it on the turntable, and then looking to him for recognition as the band stomped and swung.

"Turn it down, son."

"I love this music," I said, groveling for connection.

"Too loud, son. Turn it down."

I turned it down.

Eventually, I took all his albums, the ones he hadn't listened to in years, and carried them up to my bedroom so I could play them by myself, turning up the volume as much as I wanted, or putting on my headphones so I could surround myself with the sound. I left him sitting in his easy chair with his Scotch, slipping further and further away from me.

I told myself that it didn't matter that my father had no use for the life with which I was falling deeper and deeper in love. I hid my disappointment behind the mask of sullen adolescence. I was almost finished with high school. Soon I'd be moving on to a life where I didn't need his approval.

Chapter 9

CREEPING LIKE SNAIL UNWILLINGLY TO SCHOOL

AFTER ALL MY FANTASIZING about enrolling in some sort of National American Virtuoso Conservatory for the Dramatic, Performing and Bohemian Arts, I settled on a state college ninety miles away from home. The tuition was less than what my dad paid for my four years in high school, so he was willing to pay for this. He assumed I'd spend the first couple of years amassing my required credits for a general degree and then commit to something that he considered more practical, like a journalism major.

What sold me on the place was its reputation as a party school. I was following in the footsteps of my brothers, who appeared to have had the time of their lives there, drinking beer out of quarter barrels every weekend and attending the occasional class. I'd settle down and sober up in the indeterminate future; for now, my overall plan was to have as much fun as my body could tolerate.

Getting through the core classes so I could focus on theater was harder than I'd expected. I dropped meteorology, earth science, and math to avoid failing them. I sailed through music appreciation, modern literature, and my first acting class, taught by the coolest, most different-from-me guy I'd ever met. He was a tall, skinny, high-strung Black man from Chicago who prowled through space like a ravenous tiger, with so many ideas and opinions that he couldn't form the words fast enough for them to escape. So, he stuttered and sputtered his way through class, and his energy and passion set me on fire. He convinced me that there was no other thing I'd rather do with my life than act in plays. I was red-hot to register for the next level of acting class.

But I still had to satisfy the general requirements for my bachelor's degree, and that meant sitting in a crowded lecture hall, listening to some corduroy-clad white-haired old fart drone on about Manifest Destiny. I looked around at all the boys with sleepy eyes and scrawny beards, and I imagined where they'd be in just a few years. As soon as they completed their degrees, off would go the long hair, and out would go the canvas backpacks, the tattered blue jeans, and the scuffed-up combat boots from the Army–Navy store. The posters on the concrete walls just above the bolsters in their dorm rooms would be torn down and thrown into the dumpsters. Never again would Farrah Fawcett tease them, her erect nipples peeping out from her swimsuit, her tanned arm resting on her bare thigh, her wild, untidy locks; every inch of her urging them on: College is GREAT! You can do anything you want; drink and smoke joints every night if you want to! Live like there's no tomorrow or like you'll live forever, whichever gets you higher!

Instead, they'd be forced to settle down and do what their parents and their bosses told them to do. Their majors in business or marketing would prepare them for a life spent in cubicles. I'd sooner be dead.

(Late. The kitchen. JON, home for winter break, has been out swilling beer with his friends, and now he's wolfing down a big slice of apple pie topped with a slab of cheddar cheese, served to him by MOM, who is listening to him drone on about theater and acting and creativity.)

MOM

Well, I'm glad that you're enjoying yourself. But I hope you're spending as much time with your general classes.

JON

I know what I want to do with my life, Mom.

MOM

Do you know what I think? I think you'd be a wonderful teacher. Have you ever thought about teaching?

JON

I'd rather do it than talk about it.

MOM

I just wish you were giving yourself something to fall back on....

(1973. January. JON, along with thousands of other undergraduates, is slipping and sliding his way across the ice- and snow-covered campus, trying to secure his second-semester classes, doing his best to avoid early-morning lectures so he can sleep off his expected hangovers. He climbs the four steps in front of the Education Building, holding onto the steel rail with his mitten-clad hand. With his other hand he reaches out to grab the brass handle of the door. He trips the door latch and holds on to it for a moment. A bearded YOUNG MAN in an army jacket worn over a cheap suit is waiting behind him. The YOUNG MAN must be a business major. A flash of what his life would become flashes through JON's mind. Stifling. Uninspired. A life meant for someone else.)

(JON lets go of the door and the bearded young man brushes past.)

(For a moment, JON stands looking out at the crowds of students swarming along the sidewalks like ants in search of sugar. Snow flurries hover in the air. He takes a deep breath and walks against the flow, marching with purpose to the theater building. He pulls open the glass door and disappears inside.)

Chapter 10

MY FIRST MISSED ENTRANCE

THAT SEMESTER I GOT cast in my first university production. I crossed paths with other professional-actor wannabees for the first time. All of us had found our way to a tribe that accepted us despite, or because of, our obsession with the theater. I read all the plays I could find and signed up for all the electives that appealed to my imagination: Music Appreciation. Ballroom Dance. Introduction to Film. I was compiling knowledge invaluable for an actor. And when I was done with my classes and rehearsals, I topped off most days with frolicking in sticky-floored student bars until closing.

All that I lacked was a girlfriend, or even an occasional date. My romance with Maggie had ended in the summer before college. I had a swelled head over my sudden popularity as a high school drama star and I found Maggie too sweet, too simple, too innocent. I'd drifted into a boorish party crowd with whom she had little in common. Maggie was cramping my style.

One night she called me in tears, and I broke up with her then and there. Within the year I heard that her parents had moved to Florida and that Maggie had gone with them. I lost track of her, and our paths never crossed again.

Within a few weeks of our breakup, I had fallen for a fast-moving party girl who stuck her tongue halfway down my throat on our first date, and who later fixed my wagon by dumping me because she got bored with my puppy-dog insecurity. After the way I'd treated Maggie, I considered my suffering as karmic payback.

For the next two years I wore my heart on my sleeve and nobody noticed. I was lonely, socially inept, and achingly celibate.

But I kept getting nice roles in plays. I did my first Shakespeare scene in class. I sang a solo in a musical. My confidence swelled. I began to think that I deserved all this attention.

I also had my first experience being in a real dog of a show. Rehearsals were disorganized, the material was mediocre, and when opening night arrived, I was in a funk, knowing that I was in a bomb. On my way to the performance, I saw a Badger Bus, headed for Milwaukee, idling on the corner. I fought the temptation to jump on the bus and skip town, until my sense of obligation took over and I dragged myself to the theater.

It was the kind of play where all the actors had to make quick wardrobe changes over the evening, and we were assigned students from the costume shop to help us.

It being the seventies, and it being theater, no attention was paid to gender separation. This was the first time I'd ever been expected to drop my trousers in front of a stranger, let alone a comely student dresser. Liz wore her bright-red hair halfway down her back and sported Shirley Temple dimples in her cheeks that seemed to laugh at my modesty, and two little moles under her left eye that wrinkled when she smiled.

She wore the usual backstage blacks, but her version featured a tight braless top with micro-miniskirt and black tights. I tried not to stare. The first time I stood before her in my underwear, she cooed, "I'd sure like to see what's under there...." I reminded her that we only had thirty seconds to make this change. I grabbed the shirt out of her hands and pulled it over my head. My arms and legs told me I was all business, but I was clearly provoked in other places.

I was nineteen; I had no experience with boldfaced seduction. Was that what was going on? Or was I just imagining it? I hurried away to the site of my next entrance, secretly hoping that she'd try that again.

She did. Each night she got a little bolder. Her perfume seemed more fragrant, and she lingered over our changes much longer than was necessary. On closing night, as we finished my last quick change, she placed her hand under my belt and whispered in my ear, "I'm going to fuck you silly when this is over."

(Two hours later. JON's steamy, cramped, darkened bedroom. JON is lying on his back, naked. LIZ is straddling him, her bell-shaped breasts bobbing in time with the rhythmic creaking of the single bed's rusty springs. JON is sweating off the five beers that he's guzzled to steady his nerves. The ceiling has begun to spin. JON's confidence is shrinking. After a few more minutes, the frenetic grinding ceases. LIZ dismounts. THEY lie still.)

LIZ

(Nestling against him)
It's OK. Let's get some sleep.

EMBARRASSED, DISAPPOINTED, AND RELIEVED that it was all over, I drifted off. I woke up at dawn to the sounds of robins chirping outside my window. Liz had dressed and quietly slipped away.

A few days later we passed in the hallway between classes, and my face burned with shame. She took my hand and assured me, "It's OK." I walked away with my heart racing, but my soul quieted.

The show was over. Liz never dressed (or undressed) me again.

Chapter 11

THE CARDS DON'T LIE

(1973. Summer. A cheerily unkempt kitchen on a muggy evening. MIKEY, the tenant of this upbeat mess, is holding court at the rickety vinyl-topped card table that serves as his sideboard. There is a half-empty fifth of gin at his side. Tonic water. Ice cubes in a tin bucket.)

(MIKEY wears a silk scarf and faded Homburg even in the full heat of summer. His blue undershirt reads "Your face or mine?" He is holding a tarot deck in his hand. He clears his throat to indicate that a card reading is about to begin.)

MIKEY

> *(To JON)*
> All right, big boy, are you ready for this?

JON

> What do I have to do?

MIKEY

> Keep drinking, sweetie. Mikey is gonna tell you your future.

JON

Nothing about sex. I don't want to think about it.

MIKEY

No, no; just ask the cards a question, and then I'll lay them out and tell you what you want to know.

JON

All right…am I gonna be an actor?

MIKEY

You already are, darling. You already are.

JON

I mean, am I gonna make a living at it?

MIKEY

Let's look.

(MIKEY sets down the cards in an order understood only by him. JON waits for the reading to begin.)

MIKEY

Well, well, this calls for another drink.

(MIKEY refills both glasses and takes a dramatic pause.)

Clearly, you are going to be an overnight success. Far more successful at this acting business than I'll ever be. I'm just destined to be a tired old queen. You, darling, have success written all over you.

JON

Oh, yeah? When's this gonna happen?

MIKEY

(Staring intently at the cards)
You will enjoy a glorious success…at fifty.

JON

Fifty? That's thirty years from now.

MIKEY

Don't blame me. The cards don't lie. Drink up. Maybe you need a double.

JON

What I need is to sleep. I'm going to bed before I pass out.

MIKEY

You're welcome to join me. I've got a fan right next to my bed. And it's a double. Plenty of room for two….

JON

Sorry. Not tonight.

MIKEY

Oh, I just love to see you straight boys blush.

(MIKEY drifts into his bedroom and leaves the door ajar.)

I STOOD UP FROM the table and wobbled into the living room.

It was a sweltering night, so I stripped off my T-shirt and lay in my underwear on the single sheet that Mikey had given me on the couch. My sweaty torso stuck to the fabric. Now I was restless. I picked up a book that I'd been skimming. It was the required textbook in the acting class in which Mikey and I befriended each other. Written by the director of one of the most prominent grad schools for acting in the United States, it was considered the Acting Bible of the 1970s. For reasons that will become clear, I won't call it by its actual title. I'll call it *Acting for a Living*.

I turned to the bookmarked page and began reading. The esteemed professor, whose words I had—up to now—regarded as gospel, suddenly turned on me, jabbing his crooked finger in my sternum and lowering his voice in a threatening hush so only I could hear him.

"As for a career in the regional theater," he warned, "with a happy marriage and children, living a 'normal life': such a dream is just as much a fantasy as landing a leading role on Broadway, or becoming a movie star. Disabuse oneself of such a notion before starting out on a path that will lead to your disappointment."

I tossed the book aside, where it landed face down on the musty-smelling carpet. I turned my face to the sofa that smelled like cigarettes and stale beer. By the time the streetlights below had blinked out for the evening, I was asleep.

When I woke up the next morning, cotton-headed and with parched, foul breath, I'd made up my addled mind: the professor was a Dream Killer. And I was going to prove him wrong, even if it *did* take me thirty years.

Chapter 12

THE MOST BEAUTIFIED OPHELIA

THE FIRST PRODUCTION IN the drama department the fall of my junior year was John Whiting's play *The Devils*. Sitting in the audience, I was captivated by the woman playing the role of Sister Jeanne of the Angels. And it wasn't just because of the scene where she simulated masturbating with a crucifix. She created a compelling character, and she had the vocal chops to be heard clearly to the back row of the 500-seat theater.

When I walked into Advanced Acting class, I was delighted to see that she was enrolled too. Offstage she bore little resemblance to Sister Jeanne. Her tousled, curly brown hair was cut short, just barely reaching her long neck. She like to dress in wide bell-bottom jeans with the waist riding to the middle of her flat midriff. She favored black leotard tops, which revealed her smooth, milky white neckline. Her mouth settled in a perpetually faint smile. Her eyes had the sparkle of a person who laughed a lot. It took me three days to get the courage to ask her name. It was Anna.

Anna was twenty, just two months older than me. She looked like the kind of girl who would have been voted Class Intellectual in high school. She spoke in a sharp, forthright alto. She used ninety-nine-cent words in class discussion and enjoyed quoting Romantic poets. When she found something funny, she let loose an irreverent cackle that revealed her keen wit and impatience with fools. She was destined for a life as a character actor, simultaneously relieved and annoyed that she'd never play a romantic lead.

We got cast in the next drama department production, she as an old crone and me as a middle-aged authoritarian. We were both playing roles that we thought were nothing like who we were in real life, and we drew together in a kind of bemused bond.

Most rehearsal nights ended with a company outing to the local bar, and before long we were choosing seats at the table that brought us closer and closer to each other. We sipped Black Russians while engaging in increasingly intimate conversation.

We partnered up in scene work in acting class, and that led to private rehearsals after class, which led to eating lunch together to discuss the scene, which led to our first date, in a shabby Italian restaurant lined with Christmas lights, tables covered with red gingham, and featuring lots of Chianti. Dean Martin warbled from speakers as we sat across from each other, our faces illuminated by candlelight from wax-covered wine bottles recycled as candelabras.

She lived in a seductive old apartment building that looked like an Italian villa. One night I walked her home, and she took me by the hand to her apartment on the top floor. She put on a recording of *Jacques Brel is Alive and Well and Living in Paris*, lit candles and turned off lamps, and gently, patiently made love to me.

We spent just about every day together for the next few months. My whole being metamorphosed from a sheltered kid from the suburbs to a romantic hedonist let loose in some European village. She was Anna Magnani, all carnal kindheartedness. We progressed in advanced-level acting classes together, indulging in late-night rehearsals of the Hamlet–Ophelia scenes that we lustily allowed to get out of hand.

We'd pose questions to each other like, "Do you think Hamlet and Ophelia have had sex? Maybe we should improvise that. Right here on the rehearsal-room floor."

We searched through play scripts to find love scenes, as if other people's words would tell us all we needed to know about each other.

I went off to my first summer-stock job, and we called each other every night. In the fall, our senior year, we moved in together. By January, I was ready to take the next step, the one that all my siblings had taken, the only way I thought a relationship could be legitimized and taken seriously by the rest of the world.

We married in June after graduation, in Anna's hometown in South Jersey. It was a place that looked like Norman Rockwell had painted it, with a Main Street just a few blocks long and a Woolworth's that still had a lunch counter where you could buy strawberry phosphates.

My whole Milwaukee family made it to the wedding. My brothers and my best man donned rented tuxes. Anna wore a formal white gown, her permed hair topped by a wide-brimmed bonnet. My dad brought along his movie camera and recorded the whole ritual for posterity: the rehearsal dinner, the wedding in the local Episcopal church, the backyard reception. The weather was glorious. The whole day felt like a scene from *The Philadelphia Story*. I was Cary Grant and Anna was Katherine Hepburn. We played the role of grown-up adults and convinced ourselves that we were ready for married life.

At dusk, we boarded the Patco Speed Line and rode into Philadelphia for our first night of marriage at the Bellevue-Stratford Hotel. A month later, two thousand delegates from the American Legion Convention checked in. Thirty of them were dead within weeks, poisoned by bacteria festering in the air conditioning system.

We chose to avoid taking this as a harbinger of any kind.

After our honeymoon on the Jersey Shore, we moved in with Anna's parents, in their quaint Victorian with the wraparound porch. We slept in Anna's childhood bedroom.

I loved it. It was new, it was different, and it was rent free. We were less than half an hour's commute from Philadelphia, and Anna's mom set us up with survival jobs at the department store where she worked as an executive. There was cocktail hour every night with her parents, and sing-alongs around the piano, and weekly Scrabble games. Life was good.

For a while.

But as I climbed the stairs at night, my brain dulled and enervated by cabernet, my thoughts darkened. *When was I going to get around to finding some acting work? Why were we sticking around New Jersey?*

Soon I was incapable of stringing two contented days together. My life became all sharp edges and habdabs of tension. I wasn't doing anything to get anywhere.

(1976. Fall. The kitchen table. ANNA and JON are splitting a bottle of wine. JON is drinking most of it.)

ANNA

So, what do you want to do?

JON

I don't know. I tried grad school, and they wouldn't take me.

ANNA

You applied for two schools. There's a lot more out there. Why don't you try out for one of those?

JON

I auditioned for the top two in the country. If they don't want me, I don't want to settle for second best.

ANNA

Ok, so I guess grad school is out. So what's the plan now? Where do you want to go?

JON

I guess, New York. Isn't that why we moved all the way out here? It's, what, a hundred miles away?

ANNA

Is that what you want?

JON

I don't know. Maybe. Yeah. What do you think?

ANNA

Why don't you hop on a Greyhound and go there? Mikey's been on you since he moved there to let him show you around. I'll stay here and you check it out for us. What do *you* think?

WITH THE TIMIDITY OF a church mouse, I prepared to take a bite out of the Big Apple.

Chapter 13

NEW YORK, OR LAST ONE IN GETS A ROTTEN EGG

TWO DAYS LATER, I boarded the bus in downtown Philly and spent the three hours' travel time making lists and fretting obsessively about walking the streets of New York. I was a greenhorn, waiting to be exposed as the impostor I was.

Walk fast. Keep your eyes straight ahead. Know where you're going. Behave as if you belong there. And don't ask for directions. That's a dead giveaway.

As the bus pulled into Port Authority Terminal, I tried to silence my inner screams with the commands I'd rehearsed. But the subways were overwhelming. I paced and paused. I climbed stairs, reversed direction, looked across tracks at distant platforms, and started to panic. I was going to have to ask someone for directions; otherwise, I'd spend the rest of my life wandering through the bowels of this terrifying city.

An amiable-looking fellow in a stylish three-piece suit was striding toward me. He exuded confidence, and he looked approachable. I made eye contact with him, and to my surprise he stopped to speak to me.

Thank God, a friendly person. Maybe he's from the Midwest.

"Excuse me, but could you tell me where I can board the A train?" I yelled.

Pipe down. It's like a tomb in here. You don't have to yell.

My Good Samaritan looked around, straightening his tortoiseshell eyeglasses as he gathered his thoughts.

Listen to the man. Remember what he tells you. This is your one chance, because he won't tell you twice.

"Okay. What you want to do is go to the next platform. Just go up those stairs…"

He raised his voice slightly to accommodate the rumble of an approaching train. It didn't look like it was going to stop. Must be an express.

Good. This isn't his train, so I'm not making him late.

I struggled to pay attention, but my focus was distracted by an upraised arm extending from one of the windows of the oncoming train. The arm had been bent at the elbow, but then it straightened, and the fingers of the hand were closed on an object of some kind. The fingers released with a snap, and in a fraction of a second, I saw the side of my guide's face covered in a yellow goo. He recoiled slightly, as if he'd been slapped, and then a rancid mess slid down his shoulder, soaking into his shirt collar, spattering his silk necktie. He set down his briefcase, pulling a handkerchief from his pants pocket. He calmly removed his glasses, rolling his eyes with a look that said, "this happens all the time." Daubing eggshell shrapnel and spattered yolk from his hair, he finished his instructions, barely skipping a beat.

"Just go up those stairs, cross over, and the A's right there."

Jesus God. This is where I want to live?

I wanted to sink to my knees and apologize for ruining his day and his shirt-and-tie combination. Instead, I managed an awkward thanks and eventually found my way to Mikey's sixth floor walk-up in Hell's Kitchen, after which I spent the next three days sweltering through the dirtiest neighborhoods I'd ever seen, looking at postage-stamp-sized efficiencies with no air conditioning.

I had no idea that New York was this bleak. I was putting my life in my hands just dropping into a bodega to get some food for dinner.

I hastened down the streets with Mikey, afraid to look up, struggling to keep up the pace so the other pedestrians wouldn't scream at me to walk faster. I rode subways pockmarked with graffiti, breathing foul air, surrounded by dead-eyed, miserable people. Or maybe it just the mask you had to wear to survive here.

On my last day in New York, I kept the appointment I'd made to get new headshots, spending lots more money than I thought I could afford, and Mikey and I looked at a couple more roach-infested walk-ups on Amsterdam Avenue. I took one last ride on the tattooed subway to Port Authority, where I pushed my way through the panhandlers and the singing, bald Hare Krishnas. I climbed aboard the Greyhound bus, desperate to leave behind this bizarre city.

Skulking back to the shelter of South Jersey, I hid out in Anna's bedroom, where I staved off despair by watching every inning of the World Series and self-medicating with bottle after bottle of Rolling Rock beer.

My New York experiment was over.

Three weeks later, I got my first acting job on the East Coast, in Philadelphia, on a boat moored on the Delaware River. It was a dinner theater company that only operated on weekends, so I still had weekdays free to work at my survival job. We rehearsed on an afterthought of a stage in a monstrously outsized ballroom. The performance space shared a wall with the kitchen. I struggled to accustom myself to the sound of dishes clattering and clanging as we shouted and sang into microphones spaced throughout the stage. The acoustics were terrible because the shipwrights hadn't designed it to be a performance space. The only fringe benefit was that I could look out the floor-to-ceiling windows in the light of day and watch the seagulls swooping and alighting on the shore.

I got paid nothing for the two weeks of rehearsals; after that, it was twenty bucks a performance for being in the chorus. I got paid thirty, because they'd given me a speaking part. It worked out to about a dollar per line.

I knew I should be doing better than this.

Anna had gotten an acting job too, at another dinner theater, this one in Pennsauken. It was as crappy as my job, but she didn't complain about it nearly as much.

I clocked into work at the dinner theater, spending my weekends learning bush-league choreography and singing to a prerecorded orchestra track that sounded as if the musicians had been recruited from the local junior military academy. I was doing substandard work with bargain-basement talent. At home, I withdrew from the sing-alongs and Scrabble games, pouting in grim isolation in Anna's bedroom, now transformed from a cozy retreat to a self-torture chamber. I was a failure as an actor, and a selfish, sullen son-in-law. Down, down I sank.

It was a Saturday night when I thought I'd hit bottom. But then, I took another dive.

I'd just plodded through another lackluster rehearsal when the choreographer, who was also the co-producer, took me aside. She was a tiny tornado of a woman, with mountainous false eyelashes and a wraparound blond bullet hairdo. Her perfume was pungent enough to make my eyes water. She was so short that I had to stoop at the shoulders to look her in the face, but her low-cut leotard directed my eyes to her cannonball breasts. The wrinkled skin of her cleavage was the color of tangerine peels.

"Listen, hon, you got a nice singing voice. I need you in the chorus more than in the sorry-ass role I put you in. So, what I'm gonna do is give your role to somebody who can't sing as good as you and put you in the front row where the mikes can pick you up."

She's taking away my speaking role.

"This'll be much better, hon. And I'll even pay you the extra ten bucks that you'd get if I kept you where you are." She slung her oversized purse over her shoulder, threw me a kiss, and scampered away, shaking her tight little butt as she took the last wind out of my sails.

(The kitchen table in Norman Rockwell Village. The wine has been upgraded to a bottle of gin. JON is wiping up stray tonic water with a paper napkin. He's on his third drink.)

ANNA

You could look at this as a compliment. Now that she knows you can sing, she'll probably give you more to do.

JON

What if I just tell her no? I want the role that she gave me in the first place. What could she do to me?

She could fire me, that's what she could do. Then she could blackball me. She could tell her friends not to hire me.

Maybe I'll just quit.

And get a reputation as a guy who walks out on a contract?

ANNA

If you hate the job so much, why keep doing it?

RULES FOR ACTORS, RULE #5: There are lots of desperate actors waiting in line for the job you turn down. And if you quit, they'll never call you again.
I went into rehearsal the next day, hating myself for lacking the nerve to drop out. I moped around for a few days, and then a phone call put me out of my misery.

Chapter 14

KID! YOU'RE ON!

THE PHONE CALL WAS from a classmate from college days. We'd acted together in a few plays, and he'd been a teaching assistant in one of my acting classes. Now he was an associate to the artistic director at a professional theater in St. Louis. He was looking to replace an actor he'd just fired.

"Would you be willing to fly here and audition for my boss?" he asked. "We'd pay your way."

I was standing in the hallway, holding the receiver in my hand, tethered to the extension phone. The cord wasn't long enough to enable me to pace the floor. It didn't matter. My legs were frozen in place. My vocal cords too.

Without missing a beat, he continued. "It's an Equity contract. It's four months of work. And, of course, we'll pay your housing. I told my boss that you're perfect for the role, so I think you've got a good shot at it."

I cleared the cobwebs from my throat. "Wouldn't I have to be approved by the director?"

He laughed. "I *am* the director."

This was a theater that had a resident acting company. It was an opportunity that I'd been dreaming of, and now it was staring me in the face. I'd thought I'd never get a chance like this until I put in three years of graduate training.

"Can I call you back in an hour? I want to talk this over with Anna."

"Of course. I'll be home all night."

My hands shook as I hung up. My mouth was bone dry. I rushed up the stairs to Anna's room and spilled all the details in one breathless babble.

"That's incredible!" she shouted.

"What about New York?" I broke in, not meaning a word of it.

She looked at me with wild eyes, her jaw fixed and resolute. "This is a union job. You've got to take it."

My thoughts jumped to an empty bed and a town where I had no friends. I'd never lived alone. Ever.

"Will you come with me?"

"I don't think I should give up my job at the store just now. I can live here rent free, and we can build up some money." There wasn't a trace of doubt in her voice. "And you'll only be gone a few months."

She was right. And I wanted this job more than anything.

I flew to St. Louis on Monday, got hired on the spot, and went back to New Jersey to pack my bags.

I called the dinner theater and told Trixie or Bobbi or whatever her name was that I was quitting.

"I'll make sure you never work in Philadelphia again," she fumed.

I didn't care if I never did. I was on my way. I was going to be a real actor. With a real paycheck.

Chapter 15

HITTIN' THE BIG TIME

I BOARDED A HALF-EMPTY plane on the morning after Christmas, and by lunchtime I was in St. Louis. A volunteer from the theater met me, holding a cardboard sign with my name scrawled in block letters: JOHN DAILEY. All my life I'd seethed inside when somebody misspelled my name. But today I didn't care. I was important enough to be picked up at the airport.

I tossed my suitcase in the back seat of his car, and within a half hour we'd arrived in the quiet suburb that housed the theater. There was enough time to leave my suitcase at my apartment in a pleasant-looking colonial-style building. Inside I had all the modern conveniences: garbage disposal, air-conditioning, wall-to-wall carpeting, dishwasher. I'd never had all this stuff. Welcome to the union.

The cheerful volunteer handed me my keys, pointed me to the rehearsal hall a few blocks away, and drove off with a friendly wave. I wanted to walk so I could stretch my legs and get some fresh air. And I needed some solitary time to compose myself.

I strolled through rolling, wooded streets, comforted by the familiarity of it all. It was a lot like Milwaukee: modestly appointed houses placed a quarter-acre apart. Late-model cars in the driveways.

Cotton-candy clouds filling the sunny skies. I was breathing, deeply. First impressions are important, and I was getting lots of good ones.

A bald guy in a starched white shirt, woolen vest, and blue jeans was waiting for me outside the rehearsal hall. He smiled at me with the quiet authority that identified him as the stage manager. He ushered me in to the hall and introduced me to the actors. I tried to read their thoughts about the new guy replacing the volatile, tons-of-fun fellow with whom they'd spent the last two months.

This was the first meeting of the company since the weeklong Christmas break, and they greeted each other with body-breaking hugs, as if they hadn't seen each other in years. I stood by with my hands shoved in my pockets and a mouth-aching smile plastered on my face. The room was echoing with the sound of manic, explosive laughter. The calm, deep breathing I'd managed just a few minutes ago gave way to shallow huffs as I tried desperately to stay calm. In a room of big personalities, I was a cipher.

I had been hired to be in the touring company, which was a five-member group within the larger resident ensemble. Our job was to put together three different productions to perform throughout Missouri at primary, secondary, and high schools. There was no script. We were going to create something out of nothing, cast it ourselves, rehearse it, and hit the road by the end of the month.

The prospect was terrifying but also exhilarating. The production style of this company was known as "story theater." Its unadorned and almost stark form turned out to be the kind of training I'd longed for ever since I'd failed to get in to graduate school. We traveled with no sets except for a couple of trunks filled with minimal props, simple basic costumes, and no other production elements to hide behind. The idea was that the kids would fill in all the details with their imaginations, based on the words and actions we sketched in for them. It was rigorous physical work, and after a few weeks, I was in the best shape of my life. We all took turns adapting the material, poking around the library until we'd find a tale that seemed ripe for dramatizing, and then presenting it to the group. If everybody liked it, it would go into the show. Sometimes our efforts would lay an egg, and after a few days of futile probing, we'd pronounce it a failure, dump the texts in the trash, and go to the next candidate on the list. But even the failures were fun. And sometimes we'd come up with material that was so good that we knew we'd created something special.

I wrote long letters to Anna every few days, and we spoke on the phone every night. We started out with lofty intentions, to keep our interchanges chatty and upbeat, but over time the word content of my letters shrunk, and our phone exchanges grew increasingly gloomy. I was growing more and more distant.

I staved off my loneliness by bundling up in my winter coat most nights at about ten o'clock and wandering over to the Pub, the company bar that stood across the parking lot of the theater. I drowned my ennui with cheap beer and carousing with the resident actors who spent every night closing the place.

Rules for Actors, Rule #6: Drinking together builds a better ensemble.
Sure. Whatever.

•◆•

AS WINTER FADED AND buds appeared on the trees, I was desperate for spring. Spring meant baseball. Spring meant the end of my season in Saint Louis. I'd be back in New Jersey, unemployed, but Anna and I would be together again.

What I hadn't counted on was that Anna decided to audition for graduate school. She was accepted by one in Florida, and she'd start her training in the fall. It was one of the best acting schools around, and they were offering a good financial package. I was happy for her and yet jealous she was going to get the training I lacked.

I took inventory.

I had a good job in St. Louis.

She had a solid training opportunity in Florida.

If I go back to St. Louis, we'll be apart for eight months out of the year. For the next three years.

Is this what married people do?

Chapter 16

SLI-I-I-DE!

ANNA AND I HAD three months to spend together before the theater split us up again.

We packed up our few belongings and retreated to Madison, the town where we'd met. Anna had siblings living there and it was close to my family in Milwaukee.

We'd drifted so far apart in such a short time that we both wanted to return to something familiar. Maybe we could regain the intimacy we'd lost.

I had no chance of finding an acting job as a union actor in a non-union town. Anna just wanted to put aside money for school, so she didn't care what she did, as long as it paid. We'd have to go back to survival work.

Damn. I thought I was done with this.

Anna got a clerical job and I signed up with a temp agency. My first assignment was in a battery factory, on the assembly line. I sorted steel pins, which had to conform to a stringent weight requirement measured in milligrams.

I sat next to a scale the size of a Cracker Jack box that displayed a digital readout. If the pin fell short of 1.5, or ballooned past 1.65, I had to toss it into the cardboard box. Pick it up, weigh it, read it, drop it in the box or send it on its way down the conveyor belt. Over and over and over. Every two hours the box was filled with rejects, so I was allowed to stand up and carry the pins to a receptacle ten feet away, dump them, and return to my seat on the line. I wore plastic gloves because if I held these things in my bare hands, my fingers would immediately turn black.

The speed at which I was working was recorded. I was expected to pick up a little more velocity every hour. Ten percent the first hour. Twenty percent the second hour. I sat on the line for five hours, with a fifteen-minute break halfway through. A scratchy squawk box of a sound system played the same loop of half-a-dozen songs incessantly. I listened to "Two Out of Three Ain't Bad" and "Baker Street" until I wanted to grind Meat Loaf into ground round. I was imprisoned in a concrete-and-steel black hole choked with stagnant air and the smell of sweat and boredom. By the time the first break of the day arrived, I was climbing the walls.

(10:15 a.m. A baseball field set incongruously in the middle of an industrial park. A steel door from the adjoining battery factory opens, and a skinny young adult with a scruffy beard sprints toward the diamond. He is wearing a dull white T-shirt, baggy denim jeans, and well-worn running shoes. As he reaches home plate, the play-by-play announcer in his head takes the mike.)

ANNOUNCER

And here's Daly, up from Triple-A, where he's had a tremendous year. He stands in the box...here's the windup, and the pitch... Swung on! It's a fly ball, deep to right....

(JON tosses his imaginary bat toward first base and sprints down the line.)

ANNOUNCER

This one's gonna go for extra bases! Daly's rounding first on his way to second...the ball gets away from the right fielder, it's rolling all the way to the wall! Daly's digging for third, and he's in standing up!

(JON stands on the bag at the third base, taking great swigs of the humid air, trying to catch his breath as his scalp drips with sweat. He glances at his watch. Five minutes left of his break. He has time for the big finish.)

ANNOUNCER
Daly's taking a big lead off third....

(JON glances toward the pitching rubber, looking for a sign from the imaginary coach at first base, checking the catcher's posture to see if he suspects anything, takes one last watch for old men on tractor lawn mowers, and then breaks for home.)

ANNOUNCER
Daly's going for the steal! Here comes the throw...

(Muscles tensing, feet pounding and scraping on gravel, JON drops his right knee and skids into home with a jostle and a thump, not quite as graceful as ten years ago, but the clouds of dirt arise as he leaps to his feet.)

ANNOUNCER
HE IS SAFE!

THE CROWD IN MY head erupted into wild screams.

Adrenaline pulsed through my body as I pumped at the air with a clenched fist. And then I felt the burning. HOT HOT HOT, like touching-a-skillet hot. Scalding. I looked down at the muddied hole in the knee of my jeans, blood racing down my shin.

I limped on to the grass, plopping into the shade. The cloth covering my kneecap was torn away, blood mixing with dirt. No breaks, no dislocation, just a big mess. It was worth it.

My knee disagreed.

I doddered back to the side door of the factory and slinked inside. I took my place on the line, wiping the dirt and grass from my hands as I donned my plastic gloves. Nobody seemed to notice the dirt and blood, and by the time my shift ended, and I snuck away to the bathroom to wash away the evidence, I'd stopped bleeding. No harm done.

I made it through the rest of the week, visiting the baseball diamond every day on break. On Tuesday, I did wind sprints in the outfield. On Wednesday, I fielded ground balls at shortstop. On Thursday, I took batting practice. And on Friday, I celebrated by taking a home-run trot around the bases. Just like I'd done when I was a kid in my backyard. Once again, baseball saved me.

Because the job at the battery factory was boring enough to induce a walking coma, we were rotated in weekly shifts. In my second week, I was transferred to another part of the factory. Here I spent the first day hauling oil drums; dismantling, transporting, and reassembling shelves; and trying to look busy. On the second day, I was handed a mop and told to report to a nearby workroom. There I was greeted by a foreman, looking about the same age as me, who ordered me to swab the deck until it shone. What was it about this guy that looked familiar?

A voice called out to him. "Hey, Tim, get your ass over here!"

Tim. The picture came into focus. The long, greasy hair. The scowl. The wrinkled work shirt. This guy had been a student at the university two years back, writing for the school paper. His photo had been displayed with his byline. He wrote theater reviews, and he fancied himself an actor. I'd even read with the guy at an audition. He was terrible. And he was responsible for the worst review I've ever suffered: "In his portrayal of the young Orphan, Daly is a sickening cross between Gary Cooper and Gomer Pyle."

And here he was, working as a foreman in a factory. A stale piece of humble pie, eh, *Tim*?

But then again, he had *me* sweeping the floor.

Chapter 17

BUGS, SWEAT, AND TEARS

SUMMER OF 1978 PASSED quickly and my time at the battery factory ended. Our attempt to recapture the past by returning to the scene of it had been a melancholy failure. As I drove east and felt the strings tethering me to Madison loosen, I thought about the days I'd spent in a fog of bad humor, venting my frustrations every night over cheap wine while Anna listened and talked me through my mood swings. I was becoming aware of how much a pain in the ass it could be to live with me.

We reached Jersey, cleared our few belongings out of the attic, and took off on the road to Florida. In a few weeks I'd be returning to St. Louis, and we'd be miles apart from each other. How were we going to survive this separation? I chose the customary coping mechanism: denial. I didn't really know how Anna felt, because we avoided discussing it. Even as we arrived in Sarasota, checked into a cheap hotel, skinny-dipped in the hotel pool, reveled in a night of room service and overeager sex, and then fell asleep in each other's arms, we were already drifting apart.

In the morning, we pulled up in front of a down-at-the-heels duplex in a hardscrabble jungle of a neighborhood. The fronds from palm trees littered the crabgrass lawn. The air was steamy. Lovebugs copulated on our legs as we unpacked. I'd never experienced anything quite like Florida. I was secretly glad I wouldn't be here long.

The student housing was what we expected. Wall-to-wall, olive-drab carpeting. Salvation Army furniture. Dim lighting, occasionally broken up by a flickering lamp in need of rewiring. We subjected the place to a thorough cleaning and delousing. Anna started class. And I busied myself by breaking out my collection of baseball cards amassed during my months on the road in Missouri, retreating to my adolescent hobby of sorting the cards by teams, and playing the dice game that my older brother had created years ago. I ran errands and distracted myself with odd jobs, like dipping our cats in flea-killing baths. I drove out to a driving range to swat at golf balls to give my petulance an outlet. I was wired up with anxiety and envy.

I kept up this assiduous routine for a few weeks, convincing myself that I was useful, playing the role of the helpful spouse, driving Anna to school every morning and picking her up for dinner at five. We were living on the first disbursement of Anna's student loans. I wasn't even being the provider that my dad had trained me to be by his example; but if the kitchen was clean, the bed made, and the cats dipped, I convinced myself that my presence was justified.

One morning I killed some time at the local library. Seated at a long wooden table, I made lists in my black notebook: theaters to contact for auditions, names of friends and family to whom I owed letters.

I filled out the paperwork for a temporary library card and I checked out a couple of books. Then I placed my black notebook on the pile and walked out to the car. I unlocked the car door while juggling this mass of stuff and dumped it all in the passenger seat.

As I drove off, I glanced around at the assortment of cars festooned with bulky netting covering their grilles. Standard issue around here. Otherwise, multiple varieties of flying insects would get sucked into your engine through the grille and destroy your transmission.

Grille coverings. Cat-dipping. This is a weird place to live.

When I pulled up to the apartment, I scooped up the books, but my black notebook had disappeared. The notebook with my precious lists.

I doubled back to the library and rushed to the front desk.

"Has anybody turned in a black notebook today?" I asked, masking my panic with a nervous smile. My hands were shaking. A bead of perspiration rolled down the side of my face.

"Sorry. I don't see anything," drawled the woman with long gray hair and horn-rimmed glasses.

I muttered curses to myself as I hustled to the car. I pulled out of my parking space, narrowly missing a VW Bug pulling into the lot.

Goddam locals don't know how to drive.

My driving got progressively more reckless as my hysteria grew. I passed a car on the right, skirting into the parking lane.

I rolled through a stop sign. At the intersection just before our house, I careened over a speed bump and my head pounded against the roof. I was screaming now, sweeping into a parking space in front of our house.

I wrestled with the keys at the front door.

Once I got inside, I tore the place apart looking for my notebook. I emptied drawers, sweeping counters clean with my trembling hands, tossing books and magazines and last night's popcorn to the floor. One of the cats appeared at my heels, crashing into my ankles every time I changed direction. I shooed him away and released a spasm of allergic sneezes. My voice was hoarse from all my screaming. My jaw ached; sweat poured down my face and stung my eyes. I kicked over a footstool so hard I heard one of my toes crack with outrage. I fell to my knees, crawling on all fours, whining between curses. My clothes were covered in sweat, right through to my underwear.

I stumbled back to the car and reached into the space between the passenger seat and the door. My notebook had been wedged in there when I hit the speed bump. I clutched the notebook to my chest and hurried back into the shelter of the apartment.

Rules for Actors, Rule #7: If you should ever have a nervous breakdown, ask yourself: "How can I use this in a scene someday?"

(Two days later: The living room in Sarasota, now cleared of the detritus from JON's meltdown. Anna has a rare night off and they've just finished dinner. JON has cracked open and consumed most of a bottle of wine. The back door to the yard is open to let in the evening breeze, but inside, the air is stifling and dank. Crickets chirp from the darkness. JON's suitcase lies on the floor next to the

front door, almost fully packed except for a few last-minute items to be added in the morning.)

ANNA

I thought you were staying to the end of the month.

JON

I'm gonna go home for a while. See my family. Maybe take in a ballgame.

ANNA

You hate it here, don't you?

JON

I'm going to have to leave here sometime.

ANNA

I know you're miserable. I think you've been that way for a long time. Ever since you got back from St. Louis. You'd rather be there.

JON

That's ridiculous. My place is here.

ANNA

And you're leaving.

JON

You think I like being like this?

ANNA

I wonder if you're capable of being anything else.

JON

So, tell me what I should do, Doctor.

ANNA

I'm not a doctor. I think you should *get* a doctor.

ANNA DROVE ME TO the airport the next morning. We said goodbye. My eyes were dry and my thoughts a million miles away.

I spent a sodden week in Milwaukee, dousing my anger and confusion by closing bars every night with any old friends who'd have me. Then I packed the few pieces of my childhood memorabilia that my mom had been storing and drove to St. Louis.

Chapter 18

THE UNHAPPY PRINCE

I LET THREE MONTHS go by without seeing Anna. We kept up the routine of phone calls, with not nearly so much regularity as before. And I stopped writing letters. There just didn't seem to be much to talk about.

Anna visited me in St. Louis after Christmas. When I picked her up at the airport, she was tanned and fit. Her eyes sparkled with energy and purpose. It hurt to admit that life without me was agreeing with her.

There was just enough time for us to drive to the theater and board the van with the other actors. As we traveled through icy streets dotted with mud-spattered snow to our performance at a nursing home on the far north end of town, we occupied ourselves with airy and shallow conversation with my colleagues.

Once we parked the van and made our way to the lobby, the group sensed this was going to be a test of the spring in our collective step. Wheelchairs were parked at congested intervals, most of the occupants staring into space. The air was musty, tired, and overheated. I stole a glance at Anna, countering her anxious look with a forced smile, trying to assure her with my eyes that *it's usually better than this*. One of my cohorts, the one who complained often and thoroughly, sidled up to me and said, "I brought us a surprise when this bullshit is over."

We changed into our costumes in the administrator's office and launched into the show. Our first selection was a florid and somewhat lugubrious tale by Oscar Wilde called *The Happy Prince*. The story is about a magpie suffering during a winter blizzard, desperate to find trinkets of value that she can sell so she can feed her starving chicks. She comes upon a statue of the Happy Prince in the town square, and the statue takes pity on her and gives away, piece by piece, everything of value he possesses: his rings, his eyes made of precious stones, and, finally, his jeweled heart.

Playing the Prince, I stood on the metal steamer trunk containing our props and costumes, assuming a suitably heroic pose, looking out into the imaginary town square. About halfway through the story, I could see in my periphery that there was a bit of a disturbance, centered in the cordon of wheelchairs assembled in the multi-purpose room that was our performance space. The swinging doors to the kitchen swept open and an orderly dressed all in white hurried into the fray, her white sneakers squeaking loudly on the linoleum. I paused for just a moment and glanced down at my Magpie. The determined look in her eyes said, *Keep going*. So, I did, with a realization that our play was being upstaged by the kind of emergency that these nurses dealt with on a regular basis.

Out of the corner of my eye, I saw the nurse lean down for a moment, then raise herself to a standing position. She gestured to another orderly emerging from the kitchen, and then took her place behind the wheelchair, releasing the brakes and rolling the hunched-over figure into the center aisle. When she reached earshot of the other orderly, she whispered, "She's gone."

We kept going through *The Happy Prince* and all the way through the other stories in our repertoire. The rest of the audience stayed with us till the end.

After the show, we changed to our street clothes in silence. Anna met us at the van, unsure of what to say, stricken with what she'd witnessed. We all made an unspoken pact then and there to pretend that nothing unusual had happened. We filed into the van, and the veteran among us immediately reached into his leather bag and pulled out a fifth of

Jack Daniels. "Here's the surprise." We passed the bottle around, and by the time we got home, over half of its contents were gone. We had three weeks of bookings ahead of us; we were going to go through a lot of whiskey.

Anna sat quietly in the van, straining to hold on to a smile. I looked for the sparkle in her eyes, the glint that I counted on to convince me that we were OK.

It wasn't there.

Chapter 19

MY KINGDOM FOR A SCOTCH ON THE ROCKS

(1979. Fall. The Pub, St. Louis, immediately following a performance of Richard III. *The place is packed. A scrum of actors, all supporting players fresh from the evening performance, are crowded around the bar. At the center of the action sits the Duke of Gloucester himself. A veteran of the finest acting companies on the continent, he has been jobbed in from Canada, where he is currently a member of the Stratford Festival, on loan to the Rep to play Richard. He's casually attired in the requisite flannel shirt and blue jeans. His naturally curled coif sits like a crown on his head. He's been buying rounds for everybody for several hours, including several for JON, who is starstruck by the attention.)*

(It is closing time, and the bar has thinned out. JON has remained. ANNA has returned to Florida, and he is dreading going home to an empty apartment. He approaches the bar for another beer.)

BARTENDER

Last call was ten minutes ago. Jesus, I've got to get to bed. We've got a student matinee at ten in the morning.

JON

You're calling the show?

BARTENDER

I'm the master electrician, Jonny boy. Who else is going to do it? But listen, I'll give you one more beer. On the house. You just gotta do something for me.

JON

Sure. What is it?

BARTENDER

(Pointing to DICK)

Somebody's gotta walk him home. He's been sitting at that stool for three hours drinking Scotch on the rocks.

DICK

(Bellowing from the other end of the bar)

Ah, my good friend! The young actor with the touring company, n'est-ce pas? Come join me in a nightcap! David, give this man your best single malt, and put it on my tab.

(The bartender pours JON his usual tap beer, and then fills a shot glass with Scotch. He fixes JON with a look that says, "I'm counting on you, kid.")

WE DOWNED OUR DRINKS, and in a few minutes Dick and I teetered out the side door to the long sidewalk that led to his apartment building. He was weaving and leaning on me for balance. A blast of single-digit winter slapped our faces. We were both suitably dressed for the elements: I was wearing my Michelin Man jacket, and Dick wore a heavy army fatigue coat. The sidewalk was covered with layers of ice as well as a newly laid patina of snow. It was tough going even for sober people. Dick was laughing wildly, singing unrecognizable shanties, oblivious to my attempts to keep him from falling on his face.

After about ten steps, the ground gave way from under us. We lurched and tripped as if the sidewalk were a table and somebody had tipped it over. Into the bushes we tumbled, laughing and shouting. After wiping the snow from our faces and trying to brush the snow out of the insides of our shoes, we got to our feet, swayed back to the sidewalk, and plowed on. Only about a hundred yards to go. But before we could right ourselves, the earth moved again, and off the trail we went, landing in a hedge.

We took one last tumble in the bushes just outside Dick's door. I got to my feet and helped him up. He wrestled his house key out of his pocket, opened the door, and lurched inside. "Thank you, young man," he sang out as the door slammed on my face.

I weaved toward my apartment two blocks away, patting myself on the back for getting Richard III home safely. I couldn't wait to tell my story the next morning in the van, bragging to my fellow actors how my new friend Dick and I had had such a great time. Surely this would raise my status in their eyes.

As I made my way home, I thought about the last time I'd seen anybody that drunk.

(1970. JON and his OLDER BROTHER are watching television in a room just off the front door of their house. The doorbell rings. They open the front door, where a short, stocky man in a trilby hat is standing, his arm draped around the shoulder of DAD, who clearly is incapable of standing on his own. The man has left his taxicab idling in a pocket of the driveway.)

CAB DRIVER
Here you go, boys. Looks like he's had a few....

(JON and OLDER BROTHER take alternate sides and just barely prevent DAD from collapsing into the bushes. DAD is crying,

moaning with embarrassment, and mumbling whining apologies. His sons have never seen him so bombed.)

OLDER BROTHER

I'll get him upstairs. You get the driver a tip. There's a few bucks in Mom's change jar in the kitchen.

(OLDER BROTHER and DAD lurch up the stairs.)

I SLIPPED ON SOME black ice and came down hard on my knee. A gust of arctic air grabbed me by the collar and forced me back to my senses. St. Louis. My head was spinning as I stumbled to my feet.

I swayed dizzily. I hadn't realized until this moment how drunk I was. The one-block walk to my apartment felt like it took an hour. I fell into bed fully clothed, and words I'd read in a college sociology class rose from my memory.

"For the adult child of an alcoholic, whenever one takes a drink, there will always be a question: Am I an alcoholic too?"

I passed out before I could answer the question.

Chapter 20

SORROWS IN BATALLIONS

I KEPT DRINKING.

On the very next night I was back at the Pub, and so was Dick. The bar was quiet. The cast of *Richard III* was facing five performances in the next three days, so most actors had gone straight home from the show. But not Dick. He was knocking back the Scotch just as vehemently as he had the night before. His stamina amazed me.

He was sitting at the same stool. I clapped him on the back and immediately regretted startling him.

"How'd it go tonight?" I asked him, with a forced chumminess.

Dick looked at me as if he'd never set eyes on me before.

"It went very well, thank you."

He hadn't a clue who I was.

I excused myself and joined a table where a few acting apprentices greeted me. I bought them a first pitcher of beer and we settled in for the night.

Two hours later, I skipped home, lurching down the middle of the empty street, howling to the sky, "I'm lonely! I'm SOOOO LONELY!"

Perfectly normal behavior. I'm coping very well.

The next morning, I was clattering around the apartment, hung over again, mouth as dry as sawdust, when the phone rang.

It was my mom. She sounded calm but a little tense.

"Do you remember last Thanksgiving, when your father and I had colds at the same time?"

I freshened up my coffee. "Yeah, you both had laryngitis."

"And then by Christmas I had my voice back, but your father didn't?"

"Yeah," I acknowledged. I put down my coffee and stood at the kitchen table. I didn't sit. I didn't move.

"Well, we waited a month and then I thought we'd better go see a doctor."

Two packs a day of Viceroys...for thirty years...

"I'm afraid it's bad news," she said. Her voice was trembling now.

When I'd last seen him, he'd looked pale and gaunt. He was drinking less because his chronic sore throat made it hard to swallow. Because his voice had been reduced to a whisper, he hadn't said much the whole weekend I was there. But that was nothing new. I was used to the distance he'd placed between us.

I glanced at the kitchen clock. I had ten minutes to dress and walk to the theater.

I didn't know what I could say to my mom that would make things better. She'd been through so much over the past few years as Dad tapered off into a fog of alcohol. It wasn't the first time she was contemplating a life without him. A few years earlier, when we were having another one of our conversations around the kitchen table while I was home for the Christmas holiday, she'd asked me in a quiet, shaky voice, "Would you hate me if I left?" The vehemence of my response had surprised me: "Of course, I wouldn't." I was squarely on her side.

And now the sobriety forced on him by the pain in his throat was drawing them closer together. Still, a boundary had been set, a time limit that was uncertain yet inevitable.

I managed a few heartfelt but insufficient sentences, promised I'd call later that evening when I got home from work, and hung up the phone.

Over the next few weeks, I shambled blankly through the now-familiar routine: rising early, boarding the van for another day of shows in some gymnasium or multi-purpose room in a town with a forgettable name, followed by a long ride home, and finishing the day getting quietly polluted at the Pub. Anna and I went for weeks without connecting. I was anxious about calling her because I was afraid of what she'd say, and I was hurt that she wasn't calling me.

On the days when resentment, loneliness, and boredom gathered forces to envelop me, the heaviness cut me off at the knees. What would tomorrow bring, and the next day, and the day after that? The grumbling in the van after difficult shows was seeping into my thoughts like a toxic sludge, and simple joy or contentment was so far out of reach that I gave in to despair and emptiness.

I needed help.

But what could I do? Look in the Yellow Pages under *Shrinks*? Admit to myself that I was not going to be able to dig out of this funk without help?

After walking around like a zombie with an "I'm fine" grin on my face, I'd convinced myself that I didn't really care that my dad was ill. I had other concerns, like the job I was starting to hate and a marriage that was crumbling in my hands. A distant father was the least of my concerns.

But he was dying. And in a strange sense, I feared that I'd catch his mortality, as if it were a toxic flu.

Then came a phone call. Five o'clock on a Thursday afternoon. I was just home from work, cooking up some macaroni and cheese. It was Anna.

"I'm so sorry about your dad," she began. "This is bad timing, I know. But I've been giving us a lot of thought."

She waited for me to respond. The silence on the phone was thick and grave.

She continued. "I think we have to face that our marriage is broken. I think we should divorce."

My mouth fell open. I tried to speak, but nothing came out.

I hung up the phone and took the burnt macaroni off the stove. I cracked open a beer to replace my charred dinner and spent the next hour finishing the six-pack.

Chapter 21

THE GREEN-EYED MONSTER

TWO WEEKS LATER, THE theater's season was over, and I was free to travel. I had a choice to make: go home and visit my ailing father, or go to Florida and try to save my marriage. I decided that my presence wouldn't make my dad any better, but it might make a difference in whether my marriage survived.

I flew to Sarasota and begged. Pleaded. Screamed. My pain erupted into the kind of temporary madness of which I'd always suspected I was capable. No Daly marriage had ever ended in divorce. Horrified with the prospect of failure, my humiliation overwhelmed me. If my pride was a mirror shattered in a million pieces, I was looking directly into the shards of glass at my swollen, anguished reflection.

I split my time between standing in the middle of the living room having fits and going to the theater. There were six plays being performed in rotating rep, and damned if I didn't see all of them. Even a farce called *Let's Get a Divorce*. I laughed my way through a matinee and then screamed through dinner, trying to convince Anna to give me another chance.

"Are you sleeping with someone?" I demanded.

"That's not the point. We've tried our hardest, and I think it's for the best if we're not together anymore."

Who is it? Somebody in your class? Have I met him? Who the hell is it?

In my reckless attempt to keep myself relevant to her life, I decided that it would be a good idea to audition for the acting training program. I could enroll in next year's class. I even submitted to an interview with the conservatory director, who suggested I might like to sit in on a class and see if I liked it. On the day before I was to board a bus back to St. Louis, I found myself sitting on the floor of a dance studio, surrounded by Anna's classmates. The insanity of what I was putting myself through never occurred to me. But I had a perverse hope that I might get to see up close the very guy who was replacing me.

The afternoon session began without many of the men present. They were down the hall rehearsing as spear-carriers in the upcoming *Othello*. I watched a two-handed scene between women, one of those Tennessee Williams it's-a-hot-night-at-the-cabana scenes. The girl with the dirty blond hair, Ellen, was wearing short shorts split way past her upper thigh and a silky blouse with nothing on underneath. I'd met her at a beach outing the previous fall. She'd been with the guy that I was now suspecting of sleeping with my wife. Anna had noticed that day that Ellen was flirting with me.

I wonder if Ellen's still interested.

Anna's scene was next. She set up some rectangular wood boxes to serve as the counter of a diner. A skinny, wiry guy with curly hair pulled up a chair, opened a newspaper and began to read. They started the scene, and the teacher frequently interrupted them to give them directions and ask them questions about what they were trying to accomplish in the scene. Their words dissolved into a nebulous cloud of noise. I tried to quiet the voices inside my head so I could concentrate on the scene.

Let's see. She's got a crush on him. He's not interested. She's lonely. I guess this is supposed to arouse my sympathy. Why should it? She's leaving me.

They finished the scene and returned to their places on the floor. Then the doorway to the hallway opened, and the *Othello* actors, released from rehearsal, filed in.

I recognized him right away, even though I'd only met him once. A tall guy with broad shoulders and a crown of curly hair. My imagination transformed him into everything I wasn't: burly, macho, with an attitude. I hated him.

Anna stood up as if there was a fire drill. She took me by the hand and led me out to the hallway by a side exit.

"I didn't want you to find out this way," she whispered. "I'm really sorry. We'll talk later."

We hurried back into the class in time to see the final scene of the day.

Just act like this is all normal. Everybody's staring at you. I wish the ground would open and swallow me right here.

By the time we got back to the apartment, we had little to talk about. Anna grabbed a quick snack and rushed off to the evening rehearsal. I packed my bag and fell asleep on the couch. In the morning, Anna drove me to the bus station, and I boarded a Greyhound for the twenty-four-hour trip back to St. Louis. The long ride gave me plenty of time to think. I was sinking into depression, and I knew it was time to get help.

Chapter 22

IT'S NOT JUST
A BICYCLE

(Summer 1980. Therapist's office. A semi-detached sitting room adjoining a modest ranch house in south central St. Louis. Dusk. The wood-paneled room is sparsely furnished, but unpretentious decorating touches convey a mood of tranquil comfort. Potpourri arranged in bowls and sandalwood-laced candles suggest a Pier 1 store on a quiet night.)

(There are several features of the room that have come as a mild surprise to JON, the tall, thin, ragged-haired man wearing a stained rugby shirt and wrinkled corduroy pants. First, he is not reclining on a psychiatrist's couch, as he'd expected, but in an overstuffed reclining chair that smells like it just came off the floor at Sears. Secondly, the person who faces him in the other recliner is a woman. She appears to him to be old enough to be his mother, and, considering that JON turned twenty-five the previous week, he's probably not far off. She has strawberry-blond hair that comes to her jawline and slides backward just a touch when she moves her head in conversation. She wears a pastel-colored leisure top with matching slacks. She enjoys collecting shoes and seems to wear a new pair every week. She insists that he call her by her first name—Joyce.)

JOYCE

(After taking a moment to make eye contact)
This is what I see.

I see a vital, attractive, personable man who has spent most, if not all his life, giving away his personal power to other people. He suspects that he must do that to be loved by them.

(JON stares at JOYCE in silence, not knowing what to say.)

JOYCE

Until you recognize this trait in yourself and take action to change it, you will repeat the same behavior and choose the path of pain and disappointment over and over.

(JOYCE rises, walks over to her desk, opens the middle drawer, and pulls out a folder that holds a few dozen identical sheets of paper. She takes one piece, on which is sketched an illustration of a bicycle. She puts the rest of the paper back in the drawer, and then hands the single sheet to JON.)

JOYCE

Tell me what you see.

JON

It's a bicycle.

JOYCE

That's right.

(She points to the handlebars)

When the handlebars make the front tire point straight ahead, the bike and rider are headed in the direction required to move forward.

(She points to the pedals)

To make forward progress, the rider pumps the pedals. But, if he stops pumping, he will slow down and eventually the bike will tip over.

(She points to the light mounted on the frame)

If this headlight is working correctly, you can see where you're going, even in the dead of night.

JON
(Thinking)
Yeah, I think I got this. I learned this when I was about four.

JOYCE
(Continuing)
Now. Turn over the paper. What do you see?

(The bike is a gnarled mass of metal. The pedals are pointed in opposite directions like a walleyed pair of breasts. The light is smashed to pieces and the handlebars are crushed as if they were run over by a bulldozer. Above the illustration is written a title: THE FAILURE PERSONALITY.)

THE BICYCLE, THE MANGLED mess of metal. The Failure Personality. This is what I needed to hear, every maxim. Soon, I filtered the litany of all my recent life decisions through this funnel of power surrender. Getting married so young, longing for my dad's approval, trying to be a good husband with no idea of what that entailed, never accepting my own talent or potential for success.

A new, healthy obsession emerged: to junk the failure personality and ride the spanking-new rebuilt bicycle into personal happiness.

The first thing I did was buy a new set of bedsheets, a comforter, and pillowcases. A rainbow pattern. Bright, cheerful. Just like what I wanted to be.

Then I went out on my first date since the split-up from Anna.

Soon after that, I bought a car.

These simple accomplishments were a series of related actions; they made sense. They were steps along the way to the role I wanted to play in my own life.

These were the actions of a grown-up.

At twenty-five years old, it was time to be one.

Chapter 23

DINNER THEATER WITH DANA

I WAS FINALLY STARTING to let go of the idea that I could ever achieve a kind of career legitimacy in the eyes of my dad. Then, I found myself on stage with Dana Andrews. Here was a chance to show Dad that I was good enough to share the stage with an actor that I knew he respected.

Dana had once been a hot commodity in the movies. In the 1940s, he was a contract player with Samuel Goldwyn. Goldwyn sold him to 20th Century-Fox, and his career took off. He starred in movies with Henry Fonda and Elizabeth Taylor. He worked with Otto Preminger and John Ford. And he played one of the leading roles in one of my dad's favorite movies, a saga about returning World War II veterans called *The Best Years of Our Lives*. Dana Andrews was the real deal, and my mom was thrilled to tell me that she and Dad would be coming to St. Louis to see the play. Dad had been through his first round of chemotherapy, he still had no voice, and he must have felt awful, but he was determined to make the trip. They packed up the car with a weekend's worth of clothes, Dad's prescription drugs, and a portable oxygen tank, and drove seven hours in the summer heat.

The 1970s had not been particularly kind to Dana Andrews. He was postwar Hollywood, and the new movie royalty—DeNiro, Hoffman, Redford, Pacino—were products of a new era of contempt for authority, of questioning old norms and embracing a new morality. Dana lapsed into mostly B movies that had not aged well, outmoded even before their release. But just before I met him, he did *The Last Tycoon*, where he played a washed-up movie director given a graceless heave-ho by a young studio executive named Monroe Stahr, played ironically enough by DeNiro. I loved that movie; the script was a faithful adaptation of F. Scott Fitzgerald's unfinished novel, and Dana was perfect for the role. Sadly enough, he was playing out a fictionalized version of his own career dissipation. By the early 1980s, he'd been reduced to shambling through the dinner-theater circuit alongside his wife Mary.

Dana and Mary toured the country in a comedy called *Any Wednesday*, in which they played the two leads. For the other two supporting characters, each theater on the circuit would cast local talent, which is how I got the job on the St. Louis leg of the tour. Ironically, I had played his part at a community theater in my college town, and Anna had played opposite me. We were both twenty years too young for the roles, but we'd found that it wasn't a half-bad play. At least it wasn't cut from the mold of stale, unfunny sex comedies that most dinner theaters seemed to favor. And I was really looking forward to working with Dana Andrews and having my dad meet him.

Rehearsals began without Dana or Mary. It was just me, Jill (the other local stringer), the director, and the stage manager, who held the prompt book in which all of Dana and Mary's moves on stage were notated. We were told on which lines to move, when to sit, and when to turn upstage and give Dana the focus for one of his speeches. Nothing was left to chance or inspiration. What had worked in Omaha last week, and Odessa, Texas, the week before, was what we were aiming for in St. Louis. It was an inhibiting way to work, but it was a decent paycheck.

I just hoped that Dana Andrews wouldn't reveal himself to be a jaded jerk when I got to meet him.

He wasn't. Far from it. He was generous, soft-spoken, and charming. He had reconciled himself to the truth that his salad days were long behind him, and he seemed content with his temperate lot in theatrical life, working side by side nightly with a genuinely kind woman who had stood with him through thick and thin, and he didn't seem to mind being loosed upon an undiscriminating public who were coming to see how Dana Andrews was holding up after all these years. He appreciated his audience and was gratified that he was still able to entertain them. He'd been judicious with his money, investing extensively in real estate when times were good, so he lacked nothing and seemed to require even less.

By the time we'd worked through our week of rehearsals together, Dana had assumed a role as a father figure to me. I'd never worked with an actor as old as my dad. And he even *looked* like my dad, right down to the horn-rimmed glasses that he wore offstage, the neatly styled white hair, and his well-tailored, carefully ironed wardrobe. He even looked dressy in chinos and a cotton shirt. Just like my dad.

He took me out to breakfast one morning and told me, with an evangelistic fervor, all about his struggles with alcoholism. His candor took me by surprise, and his pride in being over ten years sober made me glow with admiration for him. I was touched and humbled that he confided in me so willingly.

As he carefully buttered his toast and added a dab of marmalade, he gave me advice.

"Always eat something before your first cup of coffee in the morning. It'll keep the ulcers away," he instructed. I nodded, thinking about the ulcers that almost killed me when I was four.

"And if you ever find yourself looking forward to a drink and it isn't noon yet, you've got a problem." It was as if he knew about my dad.

My parents arrived at the end of the week and took me out to dinner. I seized on the chance to show off, telling them all about what Dana liked to order for breakfast, and what it was like for him to play the lynching victim in *The Ox-Bow Incident*, and all kinds of Dana-inspired trivia, some of which I made up when I ran out of stories. For once, I had Dad's attention. He listened intently, but he couldn't really contribute to the conversation as much as I suspected he wanted to, because it caused him so much pain to speak. He could manage no more than a gravelly whisper, and my throat ached with involuntary empathy. But Dad didn't want us to talk about his health. He wanted me to introduce him to Dana.

On opening night, I told Dana that my parents were in the audience.

"Where do they live?" he asked me.

"Milwaukee."

"And they drove all this way? When do I get to meet them?"

It happened right after the show, in the lobby. There were plenty of people waiting around, hoping to get an autograph, but they all had to wait. Dana walked right up to my dad.

"Of course! You're Jon's pa! The resemblance is remarkable!" he called out in his hearty baritone, pumping Dad's hand with gusto.

My dad glowed. Through all the pain, all the vulnerability, all the worry, he was smiling, and his eyes were sparkling.

The two of them were standing there, looking as if they were brothers, and the wall that I'd put up crumbled. I really did care that my dad was sick, and it was way past time to close the distance between us. Dana, without even being aware of it, had, in a way, brought me back to my father.

Chapter 24

LAST CALL FOR ACTORS

TWO MONTHS LATER I was back at the Rep, starting my third season with the touring company, resuming my regular evenings at the Pub. One night I walked in to discover that just about the entire resident company was there, running up a collective tab that must have been the highest daily total of the year. They were responding to the shocking news that, earlier in the day, the artistic director had stunned his board of directors with his resignation. Over the past months, in confidential meetings far out of the range of my hearing, he had been getting increasingly frustrated with the board's ambivalence about his leadership. He was starting to sense their impatience with his acting company, that they were getting tired of seeing the same old faces in leading roles. He had done his best to keep his company protected from the restlessness of the minority, but he had grown tired of watching his back and spying around corners on our behalf.

The Pub stayed open late that night, and at bar time the lights were dimmed, the front door locked, and the reverie continued until close to dawn. I listened again to all the company reminiscences about missed entrances, onstage gaffes, rehearsal arguments, and disagreeable prima donnas. Tongues loosened, inner frustrations were given voice, and unlikely conversations bloomed.

One of the actors, Hodge, who had been with the company for almost a decade, was sitting on his usual perch at the end of the bar, his continually refilled glass of Scotch at his elbow. I had always regarded Hodge with a certain wariness, as my initial contact with him had been humbling.

(1979. A group of actors in the chorus dressing room. They are busy applying makeup and donning costumes for a performance of A Christmas Carol. *One of the actors, an eager-to-please kid, JON, not used to being with all the adults, nervously begins whistling to himself. HODGE, the veteran in the room, a tall, thin man with sharp, chiseled features and a booming baritone voice, calls out loudly enough to rattle his dressing room mirror.)*

HODGE
WHO'S WHISTLING? IS IT…MISTER DALY?

MR. DALY
Sorry, Hodge.

HODGE
Up! Up! Get out of that chair!

(MR. DALY does so, and HODGE stands to confront him.)

HODGE
Out to the hall with you.
Close the door.
Now spin in a circle.
And again.
Again.
Spit over your shoulder.
I said, SPIT.
Now repeat after me: Angels and ministers of grace, defend us.

LOUDER!

Now, ask to be invited to return.

LOUDER.

All right, Enter, and NEVER do that again.

RULES FOR ACTORS, RULE #8: Whistling in the dressing room is BAD LUCK. Don't ever do it.

Meanwhile, back at the Pub, on the night that every actor at the Rep was seeing the handwriting on the wall in big block letters, I found myself alone with Hodge. As he puffed enigmatically on his pipe, studying me as if I were an insect mounted on a glass frame, he began interrogating me. His blue eyes held me with a fierce focus, and the rest of the room disappeared for a minute. I noted, for the first time, that Hodge would make a great Abraham Lincoln.

"How old are you, kid?"

"Twenty-five."

"Piece of advice for you, Daly. When all of this is over, and it will be, soon, go far away from here. Find yourself a nice little town, big enough to appreciate art but small enough that you don't have a lot of competition, then get busy. Act in as many damned plays as you can. Stay away from the big markets where there are thousands of tall, thin men just like you. Work hard, and you'll begin to get a little confident that you know what you're doing.

"And then, in a dozen years or so, leave your little town and go to a midsize city like this, or a bigger market if you must. Then look around. You'll notice that your competition has thinned by half."

I nodded and then took a big gulp of my beer. For the first time, it occurred to me that my address would be changing soon, and I had no idea where I was going next. And it felt good. Change was coming, and I had almost six months to prepare for The End.

Chapter 25

SIT YOU DOWN, FATHER, REST YOU

AS I STOOD IN the receiving line, one white-haired man after another held out an arm bedecked in French cuffs and shook my hand. "You look just like your dad when he was young," said one. More than a few held my hand an extra beat and said, "He was a good man," or, "I'm so sorry for your loss." The somber familiarity soothed me.

At their age, they were used to this routine, spending a few nights a month in funeral homes like this one, designed to look like expansive versions of their own living rooms. Non-descript, comforting, softly lit surroundings where they gathered to say goodbye to friends, siblings, and colleagues.

My thoughts drifted back to the last time I saw him. I'd flown home in time to say my goodbyes to Dad. I got to the hospital after nightfall and waited with all my siblings. Mom offered me the keys to the house. "I'm staying here," she said, "but you should get a good night's sleep." Instead, I fell asleep in an overstuffed chair in the visitor's lounge. At five in the morning, I was lightly shaken awake by a nurse. "Would you like to see your dad? I think he's awake now."

His eyes were barely open, and with his glasses off, the swelling in his face made him barely recognizable. There was a tumor the size of a golf ball on the side of his neck. I took his hand, the first time I'd touched him in years. He squeezed my fingers weakly. I thought, or hoped, that he was offering me all the love that he'd buried for so many years, with this one frail touch. I held on to it, and him, until a flash of pain creased his face, and I let go.

An hour later he was gone, and I didn't cry until my mom, caved in on herself at the edge of the bed, began to sob. I consoled myself with the thought that at least I'd made it home before he died. At least I had that.

The sound of a distant voice brought me back to the moment. The prayer service at the wake was about to begin, and the receiving line was nearing its end, when a craggy faced man with a comb-over patch of hair stepped up to face me. His body English was sending out the unmistakable message, "I don't really belong here." He was dressed in a well-worn sport coat that looked a little too big for him in the shoulders, over a gray sweater vest with crumbs from dinner still clinging to the buttons. He seemed almost a foot shorter than me. His eyes drifted shakily around the room, as if he was already scouting out the quickest possible exit.

He took my hand in his. His grasp was firm and warm. His gaze invited me—no, *insisted* that I join him in what was for him a moment of pure, honest truth.

"Your dad was the best boss I ever had. He taught me everything I know." His raspy voice cracked. "He was like a father to me."

Before I could even ask his name, he moved on. But his words hung in the air. This timid stranger had a connection with my father that I wished I'd had. And in that moment, a tidal wave of loss swept through me.

Now that my dad was gone, the little of himself that he had shared with me would have to suffice.

Chapter 26

YOU'RE BROKENHEARTED, BUT YOU GO ON

FOUR DAYS AFTER THE funeral, I was back at work. I rejoined the company in Sikeston, Missouri, a place where Dad had traveled regularly on business. Knowing that I was in a town with which he'd been familiar saddened me even more. I was resentful that I would have to carry on with singing and laughing and making faces on stage but also grateful that I had something to occupy me, as I wrestled with the hard truth that I would never again get the chance to close the distance between me and my father.

It was a half-hour drive from our hotel to the school in Sikeston where we were playing. The morning was gray and raw. I was hunched down in the middle seat in the van, and one of the girls in the company sat close to me—in fact, closer than usual. We'd been traveling together for months, getting drunk in hotel rooms, arguing over everything from where we'd eat tonight to whether the show was thriving or falling apart. With her strawberry-blond hair, her splash of freckles under her sleepy eyes, and her beach goddess's body, I'd been carrying a torch for Kerry since the first day, even though there wasn't a chance that my desire would ever be requited.

Now I was back, and my father was dead, and I didn't know what the hell I was doing traveling in this van and going back to this stupid play when life had changed so drastically.

"Ohhh, my poor baby," she said. "Are you OK? I'm so sorry...."

I gazed around the van, full of people who cared about me, who'd spent months seeing me at my best and at my worst. They were holding me together. I wanted so much to be back home, surrounded by family, but I had to get back to my life and this was it, riding in a van to another show, one that I was proud of despite all my grumbling to the contrary, and working with people I loved, in the way that all theater people love: intimately, completely, and often temporarily. Grief punched me in the gut.

As the tears rolled down my cheeks, I turned my head and buried my face in Kerry's velvety shoulder. She smelled like lavender. I let loose a string of muffled sobs as she rested her hand on the back of my neck. This was the closest I'd ever get to her, and I shamed myself for even having that thought, but I cast aside my temerity and nuzzled greedily against her downy cheek. Tomorrow she might go right back to ignoring me again, or, even worse, teasing me when she had no intention of going any further, but for the moment I felt safe.

Over the next few days, if I didn't find something to occupy my time during the hours when I *wasn't* on stage, I'd be lost. So, I began a reading project that I'd put on hold ever since my mom had presented it to me two years earlier. It was a thousand pages long, and I'd put off reading it partly because of its length, but mostly because I wasn't moved to do so. But now I was.

It was *The Daly News,* a homespun newsletter edited by my dad's dad, a banker and amateur writer named Martin J. Daly. Every Wednesday night, from 1942 to 1946, Martin descended the kitchen steps of his home on the west side of Milwaukee to a drafty corner of the basement where he'd placed a typewriter on a rickety desk whose bottom shelf rested clumsily on the concrete floor. There he sat shivering for hours, editing the V-mail that he received every week without fail from his four sons, all of whom had enlisted in the armed forces when the United

States entered World War II. By about midnight, he had finished another edition, filling page after page of onionskin stationery adorned with its own masthead:

Published occasionally at the Old Manse...in the interest of the far-flung members of the Clan...not affiliated with any reputable News Service.

My mother, one of the millions who fought the war at home, collected these newsletters into a three-volume set that easily rivaled the New York City phone directory for size. She had more than fifty copies printed, and she distributed them to everybody in the family. My copy had sat in a bookcase for a year, and I'd barely looked at it. Now, I was determined to read it all.

Miles away from home, lonely and dispirited by distance, my grandfather's folksy news about wartime Milwaukee soothed my homesickness. My marriage had died its own inexorable death, and as I read of my dad's devotion to his young wife despite their being shunted from one military base to another, I ached to know more about him. I was reading words that my own dad had written almost forty years ago, and hearing stories about him told by his own father. Once upon a time, Dad had been young, and in love, and the same age as me. And he was right here, in these pages, for me to see. I buried myself in *The Daly News* as I struggled through the loss of not only him but Anna too.

Night after night, I sat at the tiny Formica table in my spartan efficiency apartment, stacking up empty cans of Budweiser as I read. A week into my obsessive delving, a voice piped up from inside of me.

This would make a good play.

Chapter 27

CITY OF THE BIG SHOULDERS

I MARKED MY TWENTY-SEVENTH birthday by packing my bags into the car and leaving St. Louis. In five hours, I arrived in my new home: a sparse efficiency apartment in a building next to a cemetery on the north side of Chicago. Edgewater was the most hardscrabble neighborhood in which I'd ever lived. It wasn't quite as intimidating as New York had felt, but it came close.

What it lacked in gentility it made up for in history. A block down the street on which I lived stood a one-storied, brick carriage house, where Charlie Chaplin had filmed *The Tramp* in 1915. Now it was a boarded-up storefront. All around me there was grit, legend, and opportunity. Carl Sandburg was right: Chicago was wicked, crooked, and brutal. But it was an hour and a half from Milwaukee, and accessible for an actor new to town. I didn't need an agent to audition, and I hit pay dirt early.

After I'd been there a month, I landed my first acting job, at an outdoor theater on the campus of the University of Chicago. It was my first lead in a Shakespeare play. And during the first week of rehearsal, I got a national commercial.

Every fastball was delivered to me high and outside, just where I liked them.

The bliss was short-lived. I discovered to my dismay that the theater company, one of the prestige acting gigs in the city, was a collection of some of the most insecure, dysfunctional actors with whom I'd ever worked. The drama in the dressing rooms and backstage eclipsed whatever work was happening on stage.

As for the commercial, it was shot on the morning that we opened the play. I had to eat chocolate-covered raisins by the fistful from eight in the morning till five at night. Then I went to the theater and put on doublet and tights and proceeded to suffer raging diarrhea all night, dashing to the bathroom between scenes.

But I was a working actor. Right out of the gate. I took my good fortune for granted until the fall when, as they say in the biz, I couldn't get arrested.

The low point of it all came on a frigid, windy day in November. I blanked three times in the middle of an audition monologue, and when I slithered out of the room, I opened the wrong door and found myself in the janitor's closet.

(1981. The breezeway of a Chicago apartment building, way past midnight. JON still has on his blue winter coat that makes him look like the Michelin Man, and he is struggling to engage the front zipper. He is weaving while attempting to stand still, having just left a party where he has consumed a great quantity of malted beverage.)

(A beefy hirsute bear of a MAN approaches. His smoker's cough echoes through the breezeway. He approaches JON reeking of Scotch and cigarettes, his shaggy gray hair falling in his face. He tucks his forelocks, which don't appear to have seen a comb for a long while, inside the dingy derby that he pulls down so that his eyes peek out like two piss-holes in the snow. No, he is not a vagrant about to ask for spare change; he is the director of the Shakespearean play from the summer. The OLD BOY and the YOUNG WRETCH stand together at the glass door, steadying themselves for the blast of arctic air that they are about to encounter.)

OLD BOY

How are you, son? You seemed a little doleful in there tonight.

YOUNG WRETCH

Just a little down, I guess. I felt like the only guy in there without a job.

OLD BOY

You're not the only one, son. Don't worry, things will turn around, it just takes time. I'll be auditioning folks in a couple of weeks, why don't you drop by?

YOUNG WRETCH

(Perking up)
What are you doing?

OLD BOY

I do believe we're going to have some fun with this one. *The Taming of the Shrew*, but I've got a new take on it. I'm setting it in the Wild West. Now picture this, son: a troupe of actors are traveling through the Nevada territory. They come upon an old mining town and decide to do *The Taming of the Shrew* there. They cast the small roles with a colorful cast of locals and, well, that's about as far as I've figured it out.

YOUNG WRETCH

(Lying like a rug)
Sounds great!

OLD BOY

And you know Baptista, the rich old guy who has two girls to marry off, one of them being the shrew?

YOUNG WRETCH

Yeah...

OLD BOY

I'm going to cast a woman. So, it'll be Kate's mom that all those suitors go through to get to the daughter. Kind of like a double wooing. I've got that role cast. There's this girl new in town. Well, not exactly new, she went to school here. Goodman School of Drama. She's been working in a company in Houston since she graduated, but now she's just settling in here. Damn good actress.

YOUNG WRETCH

Shakespeare in the Wild West? Sounds lame.
That's great. Maybe I'll see you there.

(Silence)

Well, I guess I'd better start walking.

OLD BOY

Can I give you a lift?

YOUNG WRETCH

Not on your life. I think you're drunker than I am.
That's OK. I live just a few blocks from here.

(YOUNG WRETCH pushes open the door. An icy wind pushes him down the street. His inner thoughts follow him as he slides through the snow and slush.

It's a job. It's Shakespeare. How bad can it be?

Chapter 28

BRIEF ENCOUNTER

RULES FOR ACTORS, RULE #9: The best way to make an actor complain? Give them a job.

The Taming of the Shrew, in spite of being one of those weird concepts where the play was set in the American Wild West, was actually pretty good. Strong acting by people who knew how to do Shakespeare. And getting cast in it was the best thing that ever happened to me.

I strode into the theater building on a bright glacial day in January 1982. The facility had once been a bowling alley; the lanes were still visible alongside the drywall borders of the rehearsal rooms. The first day of *The Taming of the Shrew* took the form of a mass costume fitting, where all the actors waited in the green room to be called out one by one for measurements.

The green room, incidentally, featured not a speck of green. Two moth-eaten, overstuffed sofas leaned sadly up against faded banana-yellow walls, and a massive black imitation-leather lounge chair pouted in the corner.

I had chosen a comfortable outfit to wear on the first day, one that would say "raffish theater guy" and "fellow out for a good time." I was clad in a long-sleeved striped rugby shirt, a pair of brown corduroy overalls, and tan athletic sneakers, topped off by a brown newsboy's hat. I looked like I was here for the first rehearsal of *Mork and Mindy*.

I looked around for familiar faces.

Nobody.

The room was full of young, handsome, carefully scruffy men. They all looked like central casting's idea of a Chicago actor: two days' growth of beard, light flannel shirt opened at the neck and unbuttoned far enough to reveal a few tufts of rugged chest hair, ratty blue jeans, and combat boots. Except for the woman sitting in the lounge chair. She sported the kind of huge-framed tortoiseshell eyeglasses popular in 1982. Her hair was dark brown, wavy, and untamed. She wore what looked like a man's wool sweater, gray cuffless pants, and black slip-on loafers. She was absorbed in a book as the conversation circled around her.

A young woman stepped into the room with a tape measure slung across her shoulders like a scarf.

"Gale, you're next."

The woman in the lounge chair stood up, greeting the costume assistant with a toothy smile that seemed to take up half her face. She set her book down on the broken arm of the chair, picked up a shoulder bag, and swept out of the room with a striding gait. I'd left my own book bag at my feet, and she gracefully stepped over it, tossing me a neutral grin as she sauntered by.

The Goodman grad.

(One week later. The woman with the stupendous smile and JON have met and rehearsed together for a few days. And now they are crowded together in the back seat of a compact Toyota, having gratefully accepted a ride home from one of their colleagues. They are both happy to escape the long walk to the "L" station, the standing on the platform waiting for the train, and the even longer walk from the train station to their respective apartments, because it's FREEZING. Not even the sunshine as sharp as a shard of glass can

dispel the arctic stranglehold on the city. The three other people in the car are engaged in their own conversation. With his face inches away from hers, and his thighs pressed against hers, he can see great puffs of vapor escaping from his mouth as he ventures into small talk.)

JON

A bit colder than Houston, isn't it?

GALE

Are you from Houston?

JON

No. I thought *you* were from Houston.

GALE

I lived there for three years. I went to school here.

JON

So, you're used to this weather.

GALE

You *never* get used to this weather.

(All the weight that JON and GALE are contributing to the rear of the car is giving them ballast as other cars slip and slide inches away from them. At least there are no pedestrians darting into the streets, dodging their way through the cars. It's just too bloody cold to be walking anywhere.)

JON

So where *are* you from?

GALE

Texas. El Paso.

JON

An even warmer place.

Stop talking about the weather. She's over it.

GALE

High desert. I'm a Dust Bowl baby.

(The car turns a corner and stops in front of JON'S apartment building. He gathers up his things to go.)

GALE

This is a nice neighborhood.

JON

Especially in the summer. Wrigley Field is two blocks away.

GALE

Do you like baseball?

JON

I'm *crazy* about baseball.

GALE

(Out of the blue)
Are you married?

(JON pries open the door, steps out of the car, and into a puddle of slush.)

JON

No, but I live with the most wonderful woman in the world.

GALE

Oh.

(*JON slams the door shut, and it squeals angrily in the bone-dry yowl that car doors adopt in the arctic air, a moan that sounds a lot like, "Jesus Christ, it's cold!" He glances into the salt-encrusted window just in time to see her smile go rigid, as if it's been frozen stiff by the subzero air. JON waves his gloved hand jauntily and turns to skip over a dirty snowbank, as the blood rushes to his face despite the cold. He immediately regrets saying the last line.*)

Chapter 29

MEN'S VOWS ARE WOMEN'S TRAITORS

I WAS INDEED LIVING with a woman. But our relationship was not the rosy picture I presented to Gale. Terry and I had met in St. Louis a year earlier, and in the fall I had moved out of my Edgewater garret and she had joined me in Chicago. We found this nice apartment close to Wrigley Field.

Terry was five years younger than me and bore a passing physical resemblance to Anna. She wore her dark hair in the feathered style favored by Joyce Dewitt in *Three's Company*. She loved a good dirty joke but otherwise moved through life with a kind of somber uncertainty, as if she wasn't quite where she wanted to be.

Shortly after we moved in together, Terry revealed to me that she had had an affair with a mutual friend in the summer. I had no business getting upset, because I'd indulged in a one-night stand while she was away.

That's the way it was with us. I had taken up with her a month after I got the divorce papers in the mail from Anna. I had been enmeshed in a series of transitional relationships, juggling girlfriends, starting new relationships before I was finished with others, and when Terry entered my life, I was still gun-shy about getting involved in anything serious. Neither of us was in much of a position to commit to a long-term relationship.

We weren't very well matched, but neither of us had the heart to call it off.

(1981. Winter. The dining room of JON and TERRY's Wrigleyville digs. It's December. TERRY and JON are drinking Irish Cream Liqueur. Christmas songs are playing on the radio. The jolly music belies the pensive atmosphere. In the middle of one of those "where is this relationship going" conversations, JON jumps up from the table.)

JON

I'll be right back.

(JON dashes into the bedroom, and in a moment re-emerges holding a small box. JON hands TERRY the box as if it contains a day-old muffin that he had bought and forgot to give her.)

JON

I...uh...I got you something.

(TERRY opens the box.)

TERRY

It's a ring.

JON

Uhhh...yeah.

TERRY

Does this mean what I think it means?

JON

(Caught in his ambivalence and turning the tables)
What do you think it means?

TERRY

(As if speaking to a child)
Do you want to get married?

JON

Of course I don't. But I can't say that.
(He shifts nervously in his seat)
Well…why not?

NO SWEEPING HER INTO my arms, no breaking into tears of joy. Not the way a love scene should end.

Instead, we just sat there, my fingers digging into the wooden table, the one she brought from St. Louis, the one I hauled up three flights of stairs just a few months ago when she moved in. Big mistake. Just like the ring.

My heart was not in this. Neither was hers.

Terry put the ring away in the top drawer of the bureau for safe keeping. There it sat, until the day she moved out.

Chapter 30

BABY STEPS

(A few weeks later. A crowded bar two doors down from the theater. After a series of timorous conversations during coffee breaks, JON has finally talked GALE, the girl with the big smile, into a post-rehearsal drink. After a few minutes of shoptalk about the play, there is a short pause.)

JON

I don't think I've ever known anybody named Gale.

GALE

My mom named me after a TV star. Gale Storm. She'll never admit that if you ask her.

JON

So, you were meant for showbiz.

GALE

I should have been an archaeologist. Anyway, Gale goes pretty good with my middle name.

JON

Your middle name?

GALE

Fury.

JON

Oh, I get it. Fury. Gale Storm. That's perfect.

GALE

It's short for Fiorentino. My grandfather changed it at Ellis Island.
Well, *they* changed it for him. At customs. They asked Charlie how
he wanted it spelled and he said "Fury." But his brother Tony said,
"No. Furey." They fought over it right there on the dock and neither
one of them gave in. One settled in Philadelphia, the other one in
Ohio, and they never spoke to each other again. I'm from a nice
Italian family. We hold grudges forever.

JON

Oh, you look too nice to hold a grudge.

GALE

That's because you don't know me very well. What ever happened
with your girlfriend?

JON

We're not together anymore. She moved out a week ago.

GALE

I thought she was the most wonderful woman in the world.

JON

She is. It's just me. It was all going too fast. I guess I need time to
think about what I want. I don't know what to do.

*(An awkward pause. GALE takes JON's hand and speaks as quietly
as she can but loud enough to be heard over the other patrons.)*

GALE

Don't lose her. And talk to her more.

JON

Damn. That's not what I want to hear.

Do you want to do something on the day-off Monday?

GALE

You do know, don't you, that I don't want to get involved with you?

JON

I don't mean a date.

Of course I mean a date.

I just thought we could go to the zoo or something.

GALE

That sounds like a date. And it's still cold out.

JON

Where would *you* like to go?

GALE

I didn't say I'd like to *go* anywhere.

I was talking to my best friend about you. I told her, "There's this guy in the play who's kind of nice, but I think he's after me." I told her all about "the most wonderful woman in the world," and she said, "He sounds like a cad."

(JON is caught. He squirms in his chair.)

GALE

Why don't we wait a few days and see what the weather's like on Monday?

Half an hour later, we were riding the elevated train together, sitting side by side, lost in our own private thoughts. When we got to my stop, I wanted to touch her, or at least fix her with one of my lovesick grins. Instead, I let my hand graze her shoulder as I rose.

JON
I'll see you tomorrow.

GALE
(Leaving no doubt that she doesn't trust JON an inch)
Sounds good.

I STEPPED OFF THE elevated train, bounded down the steps, scampered out of the station, and headed straight for the convenience store a block from my apartment. I skipped down the aisles, pulled a six-pack of cold ones from the freezer, paid the clerk with a goofy smile, and danced home, giggling in the night air.

I mean, she didn't say no.

Chapter 31

MY HEART IS EVER AT YOUR SERVICE

THE TAMING OF THE SHREW was only the second time I had attempted Shakespeare in front of a paying audience, and I had a lot to learn. Gale had more experience with classical texts than I did, and she displayed a comfort and confidence with the language that I valued and envied. She had this uncanny ability to rise to the demands of the heightened phrasing, making me understand every single word and, even more amazingly, leading me through the thoughts and images that Shakespeare had crafted. And she did it all with a passion and immediacy that felt so modern, so full of life.

Every actor in the rehearsal hall seemed to understand that she had the best language skills of any actor in the room—everybody except for her. The more we chatted about the art and the craft of acting, the more I got the impression that she found it stressful to pretend to be somebody else and step onto a stage where hundreds of people were looking at her and looking *into* her. She had an innate understanding that the best acting was deeply revelatory. The craft demanded an emotional vulnerability that went way beyond the act of learning the words and reciting them in the proper order. She brought her inner self into the work as completely as anybody I'd ever seen, and she was painfully aware of the cost it often exacted.

I was attracted to all the shiny objects that acting dangled in front of me: the satisfaction of a team effort, the attention, the creative expression, the sense of belonging. But once I'd progressed beyond the initial thrill of the outward payoff, it took me a while to understand the inner price. Gale sensed it readily. Maybe it's because she was twenty-nine, a year and a half older than me. Maybe it was because, as a woman living in a world where men think they make the rules, she was more sensitive to the everyday compromises and petty manipulations of the job. She was clearly far more intelligent, vulnerable, sensitive, and mature than I could ever hope to be.

I grew more smitten day by day. I loved to listen to her exquisite diction and crushed-velvet voice. I found her full throttle laugh infectious and electric, and I was amazed at how easy it was to talk with her. We loved the same movies, we hated the same arrogances in self-important theater artists, and we both valued simplicity and self-sufficiency in the way we lived.

The play opened to lukewarm reviews, or so we were told. Gale convinced me that reading them was pointless and destructive. If they were good, you'd strive to repeat the performance that got you praised, to the point that you'd be playing the reviews and not the play you rehearsed; and if they were bad, your confidence would deflate like a stale balloon, and you'd spend the rest of the run trying to prove critics wrong. She vowed not to read them, so I didn't either.

The rehearsal period having concluded, our days were now free, and I applied myself to some serious wooing. I resurrected my suggestion of a date at the zoo, but the weather was still raw and frigid. When Gale suggested a trip to the Art Institute, I sang and sauntered my way across my apartment for the whole weekend.

I woke up Monday morning to the phone ringing.

"Hello, is this Jonathan?"

"Yes, it is."

"I'm calling from Edgewater Hospital. Do you know a woman named Gale?"

I was confused. Why would a hospital be calling?

"She wants you to know that she's all right, but she won't be able to make your date this afternoon."

I suddenly put two and two together.

Oh my god. She's in the hospital.

"She was delivered here in an ambulance a few hours ago, suffering from an acute asthma attack. Her condition is under control now, but we're going to keep her overnight for observation."

I rushed around the apartment, scooping up the first items of clothing close at hand. I had been planning on paying some attention to my ensemble for our date, but now I just wanted to get myself to the hospital as quickly as I could. I didn't even ask the woman on the phone if Gale could have visitors.

I should bring her something. Where should I go? How do I get to this hospital? Don't think about it. Just get in the car and drive.

I drove to the convenience store on the other side of Wrigley Field and whisked up and down the aisles, looking for inspiration.

Bubble gum. Who doesn't like bubble gum? And balloons. Some chocolate. M&M's, yeah, that's it. And a newspaper. Does she read the newspaper?

I sped off in search of the hospital, running yellow lights, pushing my sluggish sedan to its limits. Within a nail-biting half hour, I pulled up to the hospital.

(Minutes later. GALE is sitting up in bed, in her private room, an intravenous tube in her arm, her face half-covered by an oxygen mask. A tall, thin fellow enters, clad in a thick flannel shirt thrown over heavily wrinkled clothes.)

JON

You didn't have to go to all this trouble just to break a date.

GALE

You didn't have to come all the way out here. I look awful.

(She removes her oxygen mask.)

JON

Don't take that off on my account. You look fine to me.

GALE

I can take it off for a minute. I'm better now.

JON

What happened?

GALE

I woke up in the dark last night and started coughing. I couldn't stop. I felt like I was drowning. I managed to fall out of bed and then I crawled to the phone and called 911. This tends to happen to me. I've got severe asthma.

(JON pulls a chair up to the side of the bed and puts a small paper bag in her hand.)

JON

They didn't have any flowers at the Stop & Shop. Do you like M&M's?

GALE

Very much. You're so sweet.

JON

And bubble gum? Do you like bubble gum?

GALE

Maybe I'll wait on that. Right now, it's hard to breathe and chew gum at the same time.

JON

Oh, right. Sorry.

That must have been scary, with you all alone and no one to help you.

GALE

I don't like being such an invalid.

(GALE says the word like she's a canceled check.)

Sometimes I wish I had someone to take care of me.

(A nurse enters just as JON takes GALE's hand)

NURSE

I'm afraid you'll have to wait down the hall. I need to check her blood oxygen.

JON

That's all right, I'd better go. You must be tired.

(JON hesitates for a moment)

Oh, what the hell.

(JON bends over the bed and kisses GALE. She reaches across with her right hand and touches his leg just below the knee.)

GALE

What are you wearing on your leg?

JON

That's my compression stocking. I've got phlebitis.

GALE

We're quite a couple.

JON

I'm not even thirty, but I've got the circulation of a fifty-year-old.

GALE

And I've got the lungs of an old lady.

JON

We're perfect for each other.

(JON walks toward the door, then turns back to GALE, holding out the newspaper in his hand.)

JON

Do you read the newspaper?

GALE

Not if I can help it. But thank you. And thank you for coming to see me.

JON

There's nothing else I'd rather be doing. And I'll come back tomorrow.

GALE

You don't have to drive all the way out here again.

JON

(One last look, as he leaves)
I want to.

I GOT HOME, CRACKED open a beer, and opened the newspaper to the comic section. At the bottom of the page was the daily horoscope. The advice to my Taurus sign read:

"Wish comes true. One relationship near an end and another is getting started. You are rebuilding on a more solid structure. You'll be happier as a result—and more secure."

I paid attention to *this* review.

Chapter 32

YOU WERE MEANT FOR ME

(Three weeks later, after multiple dates to thrift stores, Greek restaurants, art museums, and movies. It's early morning. Traffic noise three floors down. The sun is peeking through the trees. JON and GALE are in the bed, under the covers.)

JON

So, what made you move to Chicago in the first place?

GALE

It all happened because I had to go to the bathroom, actually.

JON

Tell me more.

GALE

(Sitting up in bed)
Would you like a cup of coffee?

JON

I'd love a cup of coffee.

(GALE pulls aside the covers, reaches for the blue velour robe gathered at the foot of the bed, and drapes it over her shoulders. Then she stands up, ties the robe closed, and pads over to the kitchenette. Throughout her story, she washes out two cups, heats up some water in a tin teakettle, pours some instant coffee crystals into the cups, and serves the coffee to her bed partner, who sits fascinated and spellbound.)

GALE

So, I was in San Francisco. I had a desk job in a hospital. And I just hated it. I'd dropped out of grad school in Denver because, well, I hated that too. I was in San Francisco because it was 1973, and who *didn't* want to be in San Francisco? I was twenty-one.

But one day I just couldn't take that job anymore. I went to the front office and said, "I have to quit." And the woman behind the desk— she had pencils sticking out of her hair—she said, "If you leave now, you'll forfeit your pay from the whole week, do you understand that?" I said, "Yes I do," and I got on the California line to go down to the wharf. I just wanted to sit out there and look at the water for a while.

But ten minutes into my trolley ride, I had to go to the bathroom. I looked out the window and there was the Sir Francis Drake Hotel. I got off the trolley and I walked into this beautiful lobby. Italian marble everywhere, overstuffed leather chairs, potted plants taller than you, lots of gorgeous wood trim. Voices echoing off these high ceilings. It was like I'd stepped into a 1930s movie.

But I really had to go. So I looked for the ladies' room. It was across from these gold elevators. And I saw this long table set up and this woman was sitting at it, and there was this sign: *Theatre Communications Group National Auditions Today. Please check in here.*

I went to the ladies' room and then walked over to the table in the hall. "Are there theater schools auditioning today?" And she said, "Do you have an appointment?" And I said, "No, I was just wondering who was here." And she said, "There are thirty schools here today, from all over the country. Which school are you wondering about?"

She was so condescending. I said, "Oh, I don't know. Are there any I can sign up for?"

And she looked at me like I was from outer space. "You can't just walk in. These are the finals."

I was going to give up, but then she said, "Do you see that room at the end of the hall? The Goodman School of Drama is holding a workshop there in a few minutes. You could knock on the door before they get started. Maybe they'd let you in."

JON

You just came in off the street and auditioned for the Goodman? You've got to make it past regional auditions just to get in to see them. I didn't even get past the first screening.

GALE

Well, first I had to go through three hours of singing and dancing and reciting poetry that I had to read cold. And then I had to balance this long wooden dowel in the palm of my hand for what seemed like an hour. Then the man running the workshop invited me to audition for him in his hotel room the next day.

JON

You went to his hotel room?

GALE

I went to the hallway *outside* his hotel room. Me and about twenty other people. We lined up, waiting to see him once he was finished with auditions downstairs. I waited there for the whole day. Eight hours. When he finally got to his room, we all got five minutes, one at a time, to do a couple of monologues for him. I hadn't rehearsed them in months, and I was terrible.

But three weeks later, the Goodman called, and they offered me a spot in their second-year class. They had an opening because somebody'd dropped out. So, I came to Chicago and stayed for two years. Then I got a job in Houston. When I decided I was done with that, I came back here. And here I am.

(There is a pause. JON takes a sip of his coffee and stares at GALE for a few moments, and then a sudden thought enters his head.)

JON

You mean, if you hadn't stopped to use that hotel bathroom, we might never have met?

GALE

Well…yes, I guess that's true.

(JON sips his coffee and considers the randomness of the world.)

Chapter 33

IT WAS THE BEST OF TIMES

WE'D ONLY BEEN DATING for two months, but I was thinking of us as a couple. There was no hesitation, no second-guessing like I'd experienced in previous relationships. We were a team. At least in my thinking. And Gale didn't seem to be objecting, so I kept at it.

The Great Lakes Shakespeare Festival in Cleveland was producing the American premiere of *The Life and Adventures of Nicholas Nickleby*, the eight-and-a-half-hour adaptation of the Dickens novel. I was determined to audition for what sounded like a once-in-a-lifetime opportunity, even though I didn't have the cash for airfare to Cleveland. I used my newly acquired credit card to buy us two tickets.

The only time slot available for the producers to see us was on a Wednesday afternoon. *The Taming of the Shrew* was still running back in Chicago, and we had a show that night. The weather was wretched: with temperatures in the teens and a mix of ice and snow in the forecast. Any sane person could see that we were taking a big risk. The plane could be late—or even grounded. We could miss a performance. We could get fired.

I was full of ambition and adrenaline. "Let's do it!"

Gale hesitated. I sensed she wouldn't be so hasty if she was trying to make this decision alone. But after some coaxing, she agreed.

We got up at dawn and took a cab out to O'Hare. Clear skies. Even a little sun. We were in Cleveland by lunchtime.

We found our way to the rehearsal hall and took turns presenting our audition pieces. Two monologues: one classical and one contemporary. No longer than four minutes. And then we waited for the usual "thank you for coming and there's the door."

Except Gale was in there for a half hour. I paced in the hallway. I stepped outside for a few minutes and watched the sky fill with ominous clouds that looked like dirty cotton candy. Snow clouds.

At long last, the door to the hall swung open. Gale emerged, looking a bit flushed and energized.

"Let's get going," she urged. "We don't have much time to catch the flight home."

By the time we got to the airport, the snow was accumulating on the sidewalks. We hurried to the terminal, and boarded the plane.

It's going to be fine. We're right on time.

I had the window seat. I slid open the window shade and immediately felt like I was sitting inside one of those snow globes. Men in snowsuits, wielding massive hoses, were spraying a substance on the wings.

"Good afternoon, folks. This is your captain speaking."

Why do they all sound like a cross between James Earl Jones and Burl Ives? Does somebody teach them those thick-as-syrup Southern accents?

"We're just takin' a minute to do a little deicing. Just to be safe."

All I could think of was the plane that had crashed into the Potomac the year before. The deicer had malfunctioned, and the overburdened jet went down with seventy-eight people aboard.

I glanced at Gale. She took my hand and smiled. My heart jumped a foot but not from any fear of crashing. I was flying way above the gunmetal-gray clouds.

The plane was about an hour late leaving, but the pilot made up the time in the air and we made it.

We went straight to the theater and got there fifteen minutes before curtain. We were both a little shaky and starving by the time we got back to my apartment at midnight, but fate was smiling on us.

Two weeks later, Gale got the good news. Some strong roles in *Nickleby*, as part of a rock-solid acting company. I didn't get hired, and I was green with envy. I wasn't sure how I was going to handle being unemployed while Gale served as the breadwinner, but nothing was keeping me in Chicago.

I thought just maybe if I stuck around in Gale's shadow long enough, maybe a job might materialize for me sometime. Maybe Cleveland was the kind of midsized market that Hodge had been talking about that night in the Pub in St. Louis. Maybe if I was patient, things might start falling into place. Maybe, just maybe, Gale and I would settle in Cleveland and do plays together for a good long while.

No sooner had we spent our first month in Cleveland when my plans changed. I got a job offer in St. Louis, and I took it. The pay wasn't much, but it was back in a town I'd missed. And the play was about baseball. *Bleacher Bums*. The action was set in the bleachers at Wrigley Field during a game between the Cubs and the Cardinals. We performed the play outdoors at Forest Park in St. Louis. We were all playing diehard Cubs fans, and the audience was full of Cardinals fans, so we had a fine time cheering as the audience booed and booing as they cheered.

I got back to Cleveland just in time to find out that the Shubert Organization was booking *Nickleby* for a fall run, so the Cleveland production would move lock, stock, and barrel to Chicago. Gale would stay in our apartment in Wrigleyville, but I wouldn't be there, because the theater in Cleveland decided to produce a Christmas holiday show, and they offered me a job.

Suddenly, Gale and I were looking at three months of separation. We'd already been apart for a month when I took the job in St. Louis.

This is what happened with Anna.

This time it's going to be different. I'm going to make sure of that.

Chapter 34

O TRESPASS SWEETLY URGED!

(September 1982. The corner of Ninth and Euclid, Downtown Cleveland. Bright sun. Pre-fall crispness in the air. JON and GALE are striding along a sidewalk thrumming with pedestrians. There's a fast-food joint up ahead. It has a striped awning providing a little shade, and just enough room for JON to sweep in front of Gale at just the right time. There's a slight break in pedestrian traffic flow. Go! Now! JON drops to one knee, doffs his chocolate-brown newsboy cap, and places it over his heart. GALE stops suddenly, preventing them from tumbling over in a heap.)

JON

(Getting right to it)
Will you marry me?

GALE

(Stunned)
What are you doing?

JON

Will you marry me?

GALE

I will…if you get *up*!

(He does. They kiss. GALE's face is flushed with embarrassment. Pedestrians hurry along, unaware that a future has been decided. GALE and JON duck into a nearby diner for a festive milkshake.)

BY THE FIRST WEEK of October, we were back in Chicago. On a Monday morning, I walked into the Cook County courthouse and filled out an application for a marriage license. The clerk looked at me quizzically. "You know your fiancée has to fill this out too, right? You can't just do it by yourself."

Happy with a smile as wide as my face could handle, I replied, "I'm just getting things started for us."

Before she has a chance to change her mind.

I found a pay phone and called my apartment. I listened to myself apologize for not being there, and then I remembered that Gale was at a doctor's appointment. Fortunately, I had another quarter in my pocket.

"Dr. Morton's office," a brusque voice greeted me.

"Hi, I'd like to leave a message for Gale."

"Go ahead."

"Could you just remind her to get a blood test while she's there?"

"A blood test? Doctor hasn't ordered a blood test."

"No, we need it for Saturday. We're getting married."

Hadn't we talked about this? Didn't we settle on Saturday at city hall? I think we did.

I hadn't even planned on telling my mom. I just wanted to call her with a big surprise. But Gale talked me into telling her a few days earlier.

My dear mom took the news calmly. And she pleaded with me. "Oh, please wait for me! I can take a train first thing in the morning. I would love to be there."

She sounded so happy for me. The least I could do would be to share this day with her.

Gale and I awakened on Saturday morning to the sound of jackhammers tearing up the sidewalk two stories below our bedroom. We were running late, and the sound assault quickened our pace to get dressed and out the door. We hopped in a cab, which made good time riding down Lake Shore Drive, until we got to Wacker Drive and the bridge slowly, laggardly, ploddingly raised itself to admit a cargo ship approaching the harbor. We were going to be late for our own wedding.

Meanwhile, my mom had been up since before sunrise, riding the train to the Loop, finding the courthouse, and arriving at our ceremony half an hour in advance.

(A wooden bench in the Cook County courthouse. A middle-aged LADY FROM MILWAUKEE, dressed in a powder-blue dress with a matching sweater, is sitting patiently. After a few moments, another woman joins her on the bench. The WOMAN looks to be about forty. She is wearing a white lace minidress with matching pumps. The WOMAN is holding a bouquet of carnations. The two of them sit in silence for a few minutes, and then the WOMAN turns to the LADY FROM MILWAUKEE.)

WOMAN
You been here long?

LADY FROM MILWAUKEE
About a half hour, I'd say.

WOMAN
You gettin' married?

LADY FROM MILWAUKEE
Oh no, my son is. I guess they're a little late.

WOMAN
You seen a little guy around here? Skinny guy, curly hair, bald on top?

LADY FROM MILWAUKEE
No, I haven't....

WOMAN
I don't think he's gonna show up. I knew it.

LADY FROM MILWAUKEE
Your son?

WOMAN
Hell no. Fool's supposed to marry me. I even bought flowers.

(Silence. The two women stare straight ahead. A clock ticks on the wall above their heads. More time goes by. Finally, the WOMAN rises and places the flowers in the lap of the LADY FROM MILWAUKEE.)

Here. Take these. Might as well get some use out of 'em.

(And she's gone.)

WE BUSTLED INTO THE courthouse and climbed the stairs to the registrar's office. When we turned the corner in the hallway, there was my mom. She handed me the flowers (we'd forgotten to bring any) and said, "Here's something borrowed." Then she pointed to her dress and said, "And I'm something blue."

We all walked into Judge McNulty's office. He looked like an actor cast for the role: button-downed, blue-blazered, tall, with a splash of gray hair around his temples and a friendly smile on his face. When the moment came for us to say, "I do," Gale looked into my eyes and burst into laughter.

Leftover flowers. And us laughing through our vows. It suited us to a T.

We left the courthouse as a married couple and swept over to Berghoff's for a celebratory lunch. As I pulled open the door to the restaurant, a fellow in a Roman collar was leaving. He looked up at me.

"It's Jon Daly, isn't it?"

Unbelievable. My homeroom teacher from freshman year of high school.

"What brings you here? Do you live in Chicago?" he asked.

"Yeah, I do. This is my mom and my wife Gale."

My wife.

"Mom, Gale, this is Mr. Mason."

"Father Mason now. I just got ordained a month ago."

"No kidding. We just got married, like, ten minutes ago."

We looked at each other, and ten years of history passed through our eyes. He had been one of my favorite teachers. We'd crossed paths every morning for four years, and then I'd graduated, and I never thought of him again. And now here we were, both of us having taken a monumental step in the path of our lives, sharing the awareness of it for just a moment on a busy street in Chicago. When this moment ended, we probably would never see each other again.

"Congratulations, Jon," Father Mason called, as he hurried away.

"You too, Father," I shouted over the traffic noise.

Past, present, and future, all converging on us in this one moment.

I wished my dad had been there.

The pain of his loss was fading. My regrets had eased.

But I still missed him.

Chapter 35

MIGRATION OF THE LEMMINGS

(1983. JON and GALE have been married for all of two months. They are living in a rear add-on to a rickety prewar flat in a shabby neighborhood in Cleveland, Ohio. An overnight blizzard has stacked snow halfway up the back door. GALE, bundled up in several bulky sweaters, is standing at the stove in the kitchen, cooking up lamb chops and couscous. JON is chopping vegetables at the Formica-topped table that seats two comfortably; three's a crowd. JON's MOM, the LADY FROM MILWAUKEE, is sitting on one of the kitchen chairs, the one with duct tape applied to prevent the two-inch gash at the surface from widening. They are all looking at each other from a crooked angle, as the floor slopes slightly to the east. JON's MOM betrays no alarm at the mold growing up the wall in the living room. She adjusts her glasses and gazes about the entire apartment, which is possible because the whole place is small enough that she can see all the rooms from her vantage point at the kitchen table.)

MOM

    You know, it's really kind of cute. I like the little bluebirds on the kitchen curtains. The rooms are small but...cozy. It reminds me of the first flat your father and I lived in during the war.

JON

You mean the converted chicken coop in Texas?

MOM

In Hondo? Oh, there was that one too. But this is nicer than either one of those.

JON

It's cheap. It's got that going for it. And when summer comes and we both have jobs here, we can start socking the money away.

MOM

You don't need much when you have each other. And it's just the two of you.

JON

That's true…but you know, lately I've been thinking about kids.

(There is a stunned silence. GALE looks at JON like he's let a skunk in the room.)

MOM

You have?

JON

I know. It's crazy. But every time I'm in Milwaukee, and I see my siblings with all those babies, I wonder if I'm missing something. I know. I'm an actor. I can barely support myself. But maybe it would be neat to be somebody's dad.

(GALE is flipping the lamb chops with more intensity than seems necessary. She mixes the couscous and taps the side of the pot with the metal spoon, and its reverberation bounces from wall to wall in the cramped quarters.)

MOM

When...do you think...you might....

JON

Oh, really, I don't know. I mean, we've never really talked about this.

(GALE grins stiffly and says nothing)

MOM

You've only been married a few months. Maybe someday you'll be ready to make plans.

JON

Planning's never been one of my strongest suits. And if you wait until the timing's right, it might never happen.

MOM

You picked a hard profession for having children.

RULES FOR ACTORS, RULE #10: Forget about having kids. Two actors in the family are more than enough.

It didn't really occur to me, until I brought up the topic in the kitchen that day, that fatherhood had been an idea festering in my mind ever since I'd met Gale. And it was starting to bother me that so few of my colleagues were parents.

Was it because actors themselves were children who never grew up? That the idea of being responsible for somebody else besides themselves was anathema? Or was it just because the authority figures and mentors in our profession peddled the same tired argument, that showbiz and family life don't mix?

Such judgments lost their power over me, as I perceived an openness in my spirit that I'd thought I'd never own again. I'd found a woman with whom I expected to spend the rest of my life. Not to satisfy some youthful expectation that I had to live up to, but because I wanted to be with her. I believed that together we formed the beginnings of something permanent, and it just seemed natural to invite a third party in to complete the circle.

And I was nurturing an emotional agenda. I couldn't do anything to improve the relationship with my own father, but I could make up for all the distance and emotional inhibition I suffered by raising children of my own. I would be the kind of father that I had wished Dad had been to me.

•◆•

BUT BY THE SUMMER, my focus was eaten up by Shakespeare and Shaw and the day-to-day grind of looking for the next paycheck. I didn't bring up the topic of babies, and neither did Gale. I didn't want to force the issue, and Gale didn't want to discourage the cravings that she could sense were living just below the surface of a relationship that was less than two years old. We put the demands of our careers first, assuming our marriage was strong enough to grow on its own volition.

Gale was quickly becoming one of the workhorses of the acting company in Cleveland. She had the passion and electricity to play young romantic roles and the gravitas to play formidable matrons decades older than her actual age of thirty. She accepted the latter assignments with ambivalence. She particularly resented playing mothers in plays where her stage children were older than she was. I could tell that it was taking an emotional toll. Maybe the veiled pressure I was putting on her to start a family was upsetting her. Maybe this was what it was like when actresses reached the age of thirty. I didn't know, and I didn't ask.

I had my own frustrations, chafing at playing servants with no names or characters who existed only to set up the plot before the real action began. I wasn't getting opportunities to show directors what I could do, and after I got more of the same treatment during our second season in Cleveland, it was starting to get to me. When I stopped my inner complaining long enough to contemplate the steady paycheck and the talent of my colleagues, I was forced to admit that I was a lucky actor. There were hundreds, maybe thousands of actors who pined to be in my position. But I didn't care. I was unsatisfied.

Halfway through that second season, as Gale and I were openly discussing whether our time in Cleveland might be coming to an end, our boss announced his resignation.

I'd been through this before, in Saint Louis. A new artistic director would inevitably clean house, and the present acting company would be out on the street. This time, however, there was a slim cause for hope.

Our boss was resigning to take a similar job at a theater in California.

(1983. Summer. Last call at the Five O'Clock Tap, a blue-collar bar taken over every summer by the Shakespeare crowd. The management tolerates actors because they drink a lot, and so their business thrives from May to Labor Day. The theater's boss, a tousle-haired Irishman with a pencil-thin mustache and a smile that could charm an angry pit bull, is nursing another in a long series of Jameson's. He is seated between JON and GALE. He's addressing her mostly.)

FEARLESS LEADER

Darlings, darlings, it's an artist's colony, that's the best way I can put it. A half hour from the Pacific Ocean, in a lovely area that they call the Central Coast. The lad I'm replacing has moved on to another spot, and he's taken all his associates with him. There's a school for theater training right on the grounds. I need actors, teachers, and directors, and I need them there in eight weeks. I can get you a full year of work. Would you like to go?

(JON looks at GALE. GALE looks at JON. Far away, in California, a door opens. Why not walk through it?)

We joined a half-dozen colleagues and escaped Cleveland, but not before our apartment was burglarized, which told me that our decision was the right one.

We were part of an intrepid team, and we adopted the sobriquet "the Lemmings," named after those cute little rodents who allegedly throw themselves off cliffs en masse. We were all in for whatever fate would fling in our direction.

We arrived in California saddled with an added nickname unknown to us: the Cleveland Rot. The few holdovers from the previous administration greeted us warily. The first month we were there felt like we had signed up for a one-way ticket to disaster. I was glad I had held on to our packing boxes, because I had the strong feeling we wouldn't be here long.

The first few productions in our tenure were mediocre and poorly received. We struggled to gain credibility with the students in the acting conservatory. Some days I felt like we were planting some seeds in the garden, and other days I felt like the Santa Ana winds would soon blow us out of town.

Despite all this uncertainty, Gale and I found ourselves talking about babies. I no longer felt like I was forcing the issue. No matter how strong the inner voices were telling us that this was the worst possible time to be even thinking of starting a family, we stopped listening to them and no longer worried about birth control.

Our hapless boss barely made it through a full season. He was poorly organized and fiscally irresponsible, and the board of directors quickly lost confidence in him.

On an unusually cloudy day in March, he was fired, locked out of his office in a sudden coup d'état. And we of the Cleveland Rot started thinking about packing our bags.

The next morning, I was sleeping in, after staying up late commiserating with the other Lemmings. As I rolled over in the bed, I noticed that Gale was up. I heard the click of the bathroom door opening, and suddenly she was standing over me, wearing her customary sleeveless nightgown, this one adorned with a blue floral print. She was holding a small plastic stick, on which a long blue line was visible. I didn't know what the color coding meant, but I could tell from the look on Gale's face that the world had changed.

I sat up straight in bed and looked at the long blue line. I pushed away the covers and felt a surge of adrenaline rush through my body.

"Wake up, Dad," she said.

Chapter 36

O BRAVE NEW WORLD, THAT HAS SUCH PEOPLE IN IT

SAMUEL WAS BORN ON a sunny, hot afternoon. In December. He lay in his bassinet at the hospital, a bold thatch of black hair adorning his huge head, looking for all the world like a miniature sumo wrestler taking a restorative nap.

From that first day, I was determined to be the best parent who had ever lived. I found myself competing with Gale for the prize. With every moment that I gave myself to Sam, I felt like I was building up an emotional investment I would draw on when I was old and gray, as hard as it was to imagine that day ever coming.

And there was one thing of which I was certain. I was not going to let alcohol monopolize my life. For so long I'd worried that I'd go down the same destructive path that had tripped up my dad. But now that my priorities had changed so radically, I drank less and less. I couldn't bear the thought of a hangover when I was waking up so early every morning, putting my kid at the forefront of my life. Long nights at the bar became a thing of the past, and I didn't miss those nights at all.

•◆•

WHAT I MISSED WAS a good night's sleep.

On January 2, 1987, I was experiencing the dazed, drained debilitation common to all human beings in the first month of parenthood. Never in my life had I felt such exhaustion. I was in rehearsal for another play while finishing up a semester of teaching, and Sam seemed to be spending his first month sleeping for no more than a half hour a day. Fortunately, we got consecutive days off on New Year's Day and the day after, and Gale got the idea to get away to the beach. Not just any beach, but Moonstone Beach, the southernmost point of Big Sur.

Moonstone Beach had long been our escape from jobs by which we often felt overwhelmed, and our rare days off before Sam was born had often been spent in a desperate attempt to find some peace and quiet amid the pebbled sands and thunderous undertow. At some point in these excursions, I would step away on my own for a moment of solitude, precariously balanced on enormous golden-brown rocks, gazing into the sea, willing myself to take in as much of the howling nature as I could, in the vain hope I could store all that energy away somewhere and then draw on it in the middle of some difficult day of teaching or rehearsing.

But as soon as I returned to the car, with tousled hair and reddened cheeks, all those stresses and roiling thoughts would return, often even stronger than they were before. Moonstone Beach, as much as I loved it, emitted an inefficient sedative whose effects lasted only while I could see the sea.

On this day, January 2, the scenery was much the same as it had been in our previous trips out to the beach: turquoise ocean, chocolate-brown sand, golden rocks. Purple sky. Raucous wind. I stepped away for my moment alone. Gale, by now familiar with my quirks and moods, graciously concurred but suggested that today might not be the day to clamor over slippery, jagged rocks, considering what I was holding in my arms. I paused at the grassy bluff overlooking the rocks.

Underneath my winter-weight jacket, inside the blue Snugli strapped to my chest, covered in a knit cap and wrapped in a blanket, was my son.

My boy. On his first real journey away from home. I was sharing my solitude with this living, breathing miracle rustling beneath my jacket. He was so warm! And so dependent on me. His life was in my hands.

This is what I'm living for.

This is who I am now.

Tears welled in my eyes and ran down my cheeks. It was the first time I had ever cried tears of joy.

Until January 2, I'd lived under the illusion that what I experienced on stage, as an actor, was the biggest source of joy I could ever find. But with parenthood, I found that my profession, as satisfying as it was, was only how I made my living. Being a father was what made my life.

Chapter 37

BABY, OH BABY

WHAT DO OVERWORKED THEATER people do on rare nights off? They go see plays, of course. On a cool summer evening, Gale and I sat in the open air and took in a production of the musical *Baby*, a 1980s relic about parents striving for simultaneous career advancement and personal fulfillment. It features a scene with three female characters paging through magazines in their pediatrician's waiting room, singing to each other about their innermost desires for kids, adventure, love, and more. The song is titled "I Want It All."

The truth was closer to what I heard from *real* people, who admitted that trying to thrive concurrently in a career and as a parent meant that you felt like you sucked at both things.

There were encouraging signs every now and then: the faculty member who, in the middle of the coup d'état, stopped me in the hall and said, "I hope they keep you." The set designer who fixed me with a surprised look in the middle of a tense faculty meeting and said, "You really want to be here, don't you?"

In the meantime, our living, breathing miracle was quickly transitioning from infant to peripatetic toddler. Keeping up with him was a delightful marathon. Dragging all the pots and pans out to the middle of the kitchen floor and watching him devote hours to small-motor play was more fun than I could ever have imagined. And the mornings I spent with him while Gale was off teaching were gold.

Because virtually every day was sunny and warm, we spent a lot of time outside. I'd strap Sam into the stroller and off we'd go. The park was a frequent destination, where we fed the ducks our stale bread and then scurried among Ponderosa pines, our shoes crunching on the needles gathered on the ground, taking in great whiffs of vanilla and butterscotch. As he passed his second birthday, Sam was increasingly light on his feet, and I found myself struggling to keep up with the little boy with the angelic moon face, his long sandy-brown hair rippling with golden curls, cackling and cooing as I trudged after him.

One afternoon that I had free from teaching, Sam and I rolled home for lunch and attempted a nap (Sam never was interested in sleep, especially during the day), after which we headed over to the campus of the junior college, site of the performing arts center. It was one of my favorite locales. There were long, flat expanses of green where we could run. And water fountains were spaced at regular intervals, so I didn't have to pack a lot of liquids in the stroller. The smell of jasmine and camphorweed was everywhere, and there were plenty of benches where I could rest when Sam wore me out.

On this day, Gale happened to be minutes away, performing in a matinee. She was going to be done soon, so I decided to pass the remaining time before the show ended collecting acorns with Sam.

Soon it was time for the play to finish, so I packed up the stroller and rolled Sam over to the theater.

I've got an idea! Sam's never seen his mom on stage. Let's go watch the last scene.

I scooped Sam up in my arms and stepped into the lobby.

The play was called *On the Verge, or The Geography of Yearning.* Gale was playing a fictionalized version of Mary Kingsley, the great nineteenth-century explorer. She had this glorious monologue that ended the play, augmented skillfully by the lighting designer, who had built a breathtaking series of cues, filling the stage with a palette of rich color, followed by a blue wash along the cyclorama that eventually turned midnight blue with a limitless starscape. The sound designer contributed a lush orchestral arrangement full of peaks and valleys that matched the lighting cues perfectly. Then, at the climax of the final speech there was an explosion of light and sound, then a spine-tingling blackout. In the audience, it felt like you were suddenly in the middle of space, beyond earth's orbit, beyond the stars, beyond *everything*; and then a final reveal of an empty stage, the actor having escaped quickly in the blackout. It was a fabulous moment, and I saw it many times over the run of the production.

Sam and I snuck quietly into the rear of the house. Even at two, he seemed to be familiar with the subtleties of audience etiquette. We settled in, me leaning against the wall in the center section. Gale had just begun the final monologue. Sam saw her but didn't make a peep.

We had arrived just in time to see the final moment. Gale and the light and sound board operators and the stage manager who called all the cues did it perfectly. Final phrase, stage is flooded with stars, light builds to climax, POP! Blackout! Silence. Lights up on an empty stage.

The next thing the audience heard was the panicked cry of a child. My child.

"MOMMMMMY!"

My heart skipped a beat, as half the audience turned toward me.

Oh my God, he thinks she's gone. Well, of course, he thinks that, why wouldn't he think that—she just vanished?

I hustled out the back door and sprinted straight for the dressing rooms. I got to the steel door that separated the backstage area from the lobby and punched the steel arm of the door with my hip.

The door battered the wall with a resounding whack, just as Gale appeared in the hall leading to her dressing room. She was startled to see me.

Then she saw Sam, his face red as a beet, his eyes filled with tears, his mouth gaping open as he tried to take in oxygen. His panic turned to relief almost immediately, but the tears were still flowing. Little bags of swelled flesh had formed just below his eyes.

Gale snatched the pith helmet off her head and tossed the thing onto an adjacent sofa. She held out her hands, and I loosened my hold on Sam. As Gale took him in her arms, I stood there, shamefaced, embarrassed. A failure as a father.

Within a few minutes, Sam was smiling and laughing as if nothing traumatic had occurred. But it took me several days to convince myself that perhaps I hadn't scarred my son for life or, at the very least, made him hate the theater forever for stealing his mama away.

Rules for Actors, Rule #11: To a toddler, a play is never "just a play."

Chapter 38

GEORGIA

ON MARCH 2, 1987, the front page of the *Santa Maria Times* featured a photo of the three of us, posing self-consciously on our sofa. A headline declared: "Couple Works Creatively On and Off Stage."

To people who didn't know us very well, we seemed like an unlikely pairing: me, a callow, boyish ex-cheerleader with an ingratiating need to be liked; and Gale, a reserved, mature-beyond-her-years bibliophile with a particular fondness for poetry and Regency-era literature. I loved to engage in shop talk and gossip with other actors; Gale loathed such tribal myopia, inescapable if you found yourself at any event where theater folk gathered.

But the masks we wore concealed hidden paradoxes. In private, I was apprehensive and lacked inner confidence. Gale had a well-deep sense of self and an inner shrewdness born of a complex childhood where she was alone much of the time.

Somehow, we fit together, like an enigmatic puzzle. And because we presented such a unity of diverse qualities, we didn't seem like a traditional couple on stage either.

Consequently, we didn't get to work together much. Even if we were cast together in a play, our characters seldom interacted. On more than one occasion, we played characters separated by at least ten years, and sometimes even more. In one play when we found ourselves in the same scenes, she was playing my mother-in-law. She was not amused.

Over time, the disparity began to fade. Maybe it was the happy stress of four months of parenthood; maybe it was the under-crown of salt-and-pepper hair that theater lighting accented every time I stepped on stage; maybe it was the slight air of cragginess that began to alter my facial appearance. But in 1987, when I turned 33, we found ourselves cast as a romantic pair, in William Inge's play *Picnic*. Gale played a lonely spinster, and I was her reluctant suitor. That was followed by *The Crucible*, Arthur Miller's explosive allegory of the McCarthy era. We played Elizabeth and John Proctor, a couple bitterly estranged by his infidelity and her inability to forgive his sin. As with *Picnic*, we worked with a skilled, supportive director who understood how tricky it was to portray a marriage in crisis, and then to leave the drama in the rehearsal hall, driving home to our "normal" lives as if this is what married couples do all the time.

The downside of working together was when schedules forced us to be away from home at the same time, especially in the evenings. We didn't want to work this hard only to turn over one of our paychecks to babysitters and childcare providers. And it was agonizing to be away from Sam.

That's where Georgia saved us.

Georgia was Gale's mother, a moon-faced, olive-skinned matron with a voice full of melody and languor. She spent most of Gale's childhood working as a civil servant, a clerk at the army base in Fort Bliss, hating her job, hating El Paso, raising Gale by herself after her husband left her when Gale was eight years old. She indulged her daughter in so many ways that Gale came to refer to her as "Lady Bountiful." And yet Gale ran away from home as soon as she could, at seventeen, partly to escape her mom's sexually predatory boyfriend. Their relationship was complicated, often dysfunctional, and defined by mutual dependence, unfinished business, and unconditional love.

Our first meeting, in 1982, had been inauspicious. We'd been married just a few months when Gale and I drove down to El Paso for me to meet her. We let ourselves in to her unimposing ranch house, still decorated with furniture purchased in the early 1960s, to find her on the sofa, dressed in well-worn bedclothes, surrounded by books, old newspapers, dirty dishes, and cups stained with the dregs of several mornings' worth of coffee. Without getting up, she held out her hand and offered me a warm smile. Then she settled back into the sofa.

"Is she alright?" I asked Gale, once we were alone.

"Oh, she's fine," Gale assured me. "That's probably all we'll see of her till tomorrow. I know that look. She won't get up from that sofa for the rest of the day. But don't worry. She really likes you. I can see it in her eyes."

It took me only a few days in El Paso to see that Gale hadn't been exaggerating about her difficult childhood. But Georgia's unguarded kindness toward me convinced me that I had passed whatever test she might have devised. She trusted me with her daughter, who was clearly the most important person in her life.

So, when we asked her in 1987 if she'd be willing to fly out to California from time to time and help us with childcare, she leaped at the opportunity.

Thanks to Georgia, we had it all figured out.

(1990. Easter Sunday. JON and GALE's treehouse apartment. Phone rings. GALE takes the wireless phone off its crib and sits at the table, looking out at the jacaranda in the backyard. JON and SAM are playing with Legos on the kitchen floor.)

GALE
    Hello?

MALE VOICE
    Is this Gale?

GALE
    Yes, it is.

DOCTOR
    This is Dr. Fuentes at El Paso General Hospital.

GALE

Oh dear.

DOCTOR

We admitted your mother this morning. She experienced chest pains last night as she was flying home from seeing you.

GALE

(Sitting stock still)

Is she all right?

DOCTOR

She's sleeping now. She's had a rough few hours. She woke up this morning with more chest pains and drove all the way across town to her doctor—

GALE

(Biting her lip)

Dr. *Clay.*

DOCTOR

He suggested she go to the hospital.

GALE

She *drove?*

DOCTOR

(Acknowledging the obvious)

Your mother is one tough lady.

GALE

Yes, she is.

(She grabs JON's hand and squeezes it hard.)

DOCTOR

We've scheduled her for bypass surgery tomorrow morning. She's not quite stable enough for an operation right now. We want to wait until her blood pressure levels drop a little. But that'll give you time to get here from—where are you? California?

(SAM and DAD are standing at her side. GALE thanks the DOCTOR and presses the OFF button on the phone.)

JON

Is it Georgia?

GALE

She looked pale when she left yesterday. And that pill-pushing doctor of hers didn't lift a finger.

JON

So, what do we do?

GALE

He told me to come. Today.

JON

Sam, do you want to fly in a plane?

SAM

(Trying out a new word)
That sounds instristing.

(Next morning. El Paso. Hospital room. GEORGIA is sitting up. Color has returned to her face. Her elegantly long fingernails are painted flawlessly in Aztec orange. She is reciting a litany of instructions for GALE and JON to follow in case the surgery yields unfavorable consequences.)

GEORGIA

My wedding rings and my grandmother's diamonds are in my bedroom. No one could ever find them, so I'm going to tell you where they are.

GALE

Everything's going to be all right, Mom.

GEORGIA

They're inside the doorknobs of the closet. And the rubies, they're in the light fixture in the kitchen.

GALE

Mom...

GEORGIA

I love you, my Princess of Sweet Delight. Don't worry.

(Next morning. GALE and JON are sitting at a table in GEORGIA's backyard. They are smoking Marlboro Lights. Neither of them has smoked in five years. The phone rings. It's the doctor calling from the hospital.)

DOCTOR

I'm afraid I have difficult news. Your mother had a rather serious stroke while we were operating.

(GALE stubs out her Marlboro Light, picks up her half-filled coffee cup, and takes JON's hand. They both stand up; GALE drops JON's hand to open the screen door, and they walk into the kitchen. SAM is playing with pots and pans.)

GALE

Come on, baby. We're going to see Grandma.

(No tears. No raised voices. GALE is calm and alert. Within minutes, they have driven across town to the hospital and are sitting in one of those sterile, cheerless lounge areas where families and doctors gather at times such as these. The doctor who is talking to GALE and JON looks like a clone of Dan Quayle, which makes them immediately dislike him.)

DAN QUAYLE

She's partially paralyzed right now, but we're hoping she'll get most of that back over the next few days. What I'm really concerned about is her cognitive ability.

GALE

Can she talk?

DAN QUAYLE

Yes. We asked her a few questions. Her name. She got that right. We asked her who was the president, and she said "Kennedy."

You should be prepared for significant cognitive dysfunction. I don't expect her to be able to live alone. She has at least a month of institutional therapy ahead of her. And even after that, I think it'll be very difficult for you to provide her with adequate care. If I were you, I'd start investigating nursing care in a permanent facility.

MY THOUGHTS ROILED WITH dislike toward this guy. And not just because he looked like Dan Quayle. He was telling us to put her away in a home, to dispose of Georgia as if she were a piece of broken furniture. Maybe that's what Dan would do, but not us.

(Two hours later. JON parks the car in Georgia's garage, and they walk in through the side door to the kitchen area. The cupboards are wide open, food is splayed out on the table. There is a broken window. GALE is looking out into the backyard through shards of glass.)

JON

(After a peremptory search)
Must have been kids. All they took was a pizza from the freezer and
a couple of beers. At least they didn't look in the doorknobs.

*(GALE is not laughing. JON shuts the hell up and goes to clean up
the mess.)*

WE SPENT THE NEXT three weeks in El Paso, waiting for Georgia
to be strong enough to handle being transferred to a rehabilitation
hospital. Again, Dan Quayle lobbied us to put her in a nursing home,
but we were determined to do the right thing, even though we hadn't the
slightest idea how to care for a woman with irreparable brain damage.
We would buy a house in California, one with an extra bedroom for
Georgia. She would come live with us. I owed it to Georgia, after all she'd
done for us over the last three years.

I'd watched my mom take care of my dad the last years of his life. And
being the child of an alcoholic, I wouldn't let myself rest until I'd fixed the
problem. I remembered the two months when I was in college and I was
stuck in my apartment for two weeks waiting for a blood clot in my leg to
dissolve, and my big brother and his wife took care of me, visiting me every
day, bringing me food, making sure I was taking my medication. If family
was as important to me as I professed it was, I had no choice in the matter. I
would do the right thing, even if I didn't exactly know what that was just yet.

We put Georgia's house on the market, got her temporarily settled
in the rehab center in El Paso, and flew back in time to start rehearsals
for our next play: *Much Ado About Nothing.* The turn our lives was taking
was anything but that.

Chapter 39

I DO LOVE NOTHING IN THE WORLD SO WELL AS YOU

THE FIRST DAYS OF rehearsals for *Much Ado About Nothing* were not the usual mix of manic energy and middling anxiety. It was more like stretching out amid the hushed pulse of a whirlpool bath. All our colleagues were aware of the pressure that Gale and I were under at home. We sat at a table, miles away from our responsibilities, losing ourselves in Shakespeare's language, and then acting out a captivating story where our characters were flirting, fighting, courting, and finally falling madly in love. The onstage love affair reminded me of why I fell in love with Gale in the first place.

Shakespeare was helping me to retrace the steps that brought us together in real life. Our director, who was also our boss at the Conservatory, our most staunch advocate, and becoming one of our dearest friends was gracious, patient, and glad to give us the opportunity to escape our lives for a few hours a day. We had no shortage of childcare; our students needed money and jumped at the opportunity to sit with Sam while we worked. We were keeping our heads about us, for now.

We'd been in rehearsals for almost a month when Dan Quayle called from El Paso to check on us.

"Have you placed her in a nursing home yet?" He hadn't changed his tune.

No. We bought a one-way airfare for Georgia, hired a nurse to put her on the plane, and picked her up at the Santa Barbara airport. She didn't look terribly different from the woman we'd put on a plane a month ago, but over the next few weeks it became clear just how much damage she had suffered and that much of it was irreversible. She could answer simple questions when we asked them, but her ability to initiate conversation was gone. She looked at books that we gave her to read, but she didn't remember any of their content. She had to be reminded to eat the food put in front of her, to take her pills, and to brush her teeth in the morning. She could identify us by name, but her long-term memories had either faded to vague shadows or were of no interest to her anymore. She never talked about the past, and she couldn't hold on to events that had taken place only hours ago.

We could look in her eyes, we could hear her speak. We could smell the perfume that Gale had dabbed just below her ear; and yet something deeply personal to her, something that defined her and made her Georgia, was missing, and it wasn't going to come back. Gale hadn't technically lost her mother as we'd feared she might, but the essence of her, what made her Georgia, was gone.

I watched helplessly as Gale grieved for her mother, even though Georgia, or at least a part of her, was still alive. It was a profound grief, fueled by guilt, loss, and an anguishing dread that we weren't up to the task that we'd shouldered.

Some days it felt sadder than death, and I wondered if Georgia herself was grieving for what she'd lost.

One day I walked into rehearsal, ready to work. I presumed that my mask was in place, the one that says all is well if you don't press for details. I caught the eye of one of the actors, the woman who had played the young Abigail who had seduced John Proctor into infidelity in *The Crucible*. She walked over to me and opened her arms. Before we made contact, I crumbled from a part of me that was so deep it shocked me. If we touched, if we even came close, I would be a puddle of sorrow on the floor. I had a job to do, and I'd be useless at it if I gave in to my grief even for a moment. I was a tangled network of tension and force of will, and the electrical charge in my nerves was holding me together.

I stiffened up as if I'd taken in a few thousand volts, and I backed away. *Sorry. No offense, but don't touch me.*

From El Paso came the word that Georgia's house sold. The new owners wanted to move in at the end of the month. That gave us about two weeks. *Much Ado About Nothing* had just opened and been inserted into the rotation of the summer season; I had about two and a half days between performances. Sixty hours. I woke at dawn, drove a U-Haul to El Paso, and started sorting through furniture and clothes and packing up Georgia's possessions.

I stepped into the 1965 time capsule that was Georgia's house. She probably hadn't thrown anything away since then. I had to be brutal, relentless, and decisive. After staying up all night emptying closets and dressers that looked as if they hadn't been touched in years, I called St. Vincent de Paul, and the movers came and carted away everything that was salvageable: roomfuls of furniture, closets full of clothes, appliances. I was dismantling Georgia's life. I would have been eaten up with guilt if I hadn't been so stressed out and sleep deprived. What business was it of mine to wipe this place clean of any trace that she had once lived here?

Just before dawn the following morning, I drove away from the shell of Georgia's life with the jewels and rubies from the doorknobs and light fixtures safely stowed in my backpack. I retraced my route of thirty-six hours ago across the desert, back to California, guzzling Diet Coke and munching Hostess Fruit Pies to keep me awake. I was beyond exhaustion, giddy and hysterical with adrenaline and caffeine when I pulled up in front of our apartment with just enough time to shower, shave, and hurry to the evening performance of *Much Ado.*

I was attempting to do something ridiculous, reckless, and even dangerous. I was about to spend three hours capering about the stage, bounding up stairs to platforms twenty feet above the floor, filling a four-hundred-seat house with my voice, playing boisterous comedy and heart-aching drama, all of it opposite a scene partner who was just as exhausted as I was, grieving over her mother while agonizing over leaving her child with a babysitter all night.

Must the show go on? Really?

As I hurriedly threw on my costume for Act One, manic energy bustled inside of me. The adrenaline was kicking in, and I couldn't wait to get on stage. If I stopped to really think about what I was doing, I felt like I would either begin crying hysterically or laughing and not being able to stop. I hadn't felt this way since the snowy afternoon ten years ago, as I rode through Nowhere, Missouri, in a van with a bunch of actors, getting ready to perform the night after burying my dad.

The show must go on. What a ridiculous idea.

And yet, this was what was getting me through it all. I had a job to do. A job that, for all its impossible demands, I loved.

The last scene of *Much Ado About Nothing* involved the entire company, all of us dressed for a formal celebration of Benedick and Beatrice's nuptials. When the final words of the text had been spoken, the strains of Massenet's "Méditation" from his opera *Thaïs*, a rapturously ardent piece of music, filled the theater. Gale and I stepped downstage to a portico; the audience was close enough to touch us. Our evening's work done, all that was left to do was to hold on to each other, dance to the soul-stirring melody, and then engage in a passionate kiss as the lights faded to black. For a precious moment all fears, all suffering, all pain slipped away into the night. We were safe, content, and in love. Newlyweds again.

Rules for Actors, Rule #12: Maybe the show doesn't have to go on. But sometimes it saves us.

Chapter 40

MY MIND IS TOSSING ON THE OCEAN

BUT MY LIFE WASN'T a play. I had to strip off my fancy clothes, wash off the makeup, put on my sweatshirt and jeans, lace up my sneakers, and hurry home to responsibilities that some days were overwhelming. Just when I started to think that I was getting fatherhood figured out, I was suddenly looking after a grown woman who had to be reminded to go to the bathroom. It often felt like I was taking care of two children: one who was growing up before my eyes, and one who was likely to grow even more dependent over time.

At first, I thought that it would be enough to keep her fed, engaged, and as independent as she could manage. But soon it became a day-to-day struggle just to keep her safe.

When Georgia first moved in with us, I made it a point to spend some time taking a walk with her in the neighborhood. The sidewalks were smooth and wide, there were lots of gardens and flower beds and trees to look at, and of course the weather was always perfect. Two months in, I abandoned my goal to manage a walk around the block, and in three months our walks had degraded from half a block to three houses and back, to just the length of our small front yard.

One morning she abruptly stopped after taking ten steps, bending over at the waist and gasping for breath, her quivering voice begging me: "I can't…I can't…take me home…." I put my arm around her waist, telling myself not to panic. Just get her home. I started to ease her to move, as if I was leading her in a slow dance toward safety. But she just stood motionless, staring at the sidewalk, voicing her fear in sighs and whimpers. It felt like she had forgotten how to walk, and we were both just stuck there in a terrifying standstill. Her wrists and arms were trembling. Her pulse was racing. "Just breathe, Georgia," I begged, and after a few moments she looked up at me, anguish in her eyes. And then we began a careful shuffle back to the house.

I pried open the screen door with my left hand. By this time, Georgia had shifted all her weight so she was caving on to my right side. I lowered my hip to accept her full weight and bent at my knees so that we'd keep our balance. We stepped into the room. A lounge chair was mere steps away.

I guided her over to the chair. My back was roaring its disapproval as I bent myself in knots trying to keep us from falling.

When we reached the overstuffed chair, she fell into it with such force that I thought I heard the frame snap. But she was safe.

Six months went by before it occurred to me that we weren't going on family outings anymore. One of us was always staying home with Georgia. Trips to the zoo, or Disneyland, or the beach had been highlights of our busy lives, and now we were simply doing without. It was a price we were paying that I hadn't expected, and it was too late to turn back.

The school year began at the acting conservatory, and we were needed at an emergency meeting of the faculty. "It'll only take an hour, but it's important that you're both there," our boss told us. Sam was at preschool, so we didn't have to pick him up until later.

"What could happen in an hour?" I reasoned to myself. I set up Georgia in bed with some large-print books (she was going through three every week before we noticed that her brain wasn't retaining any of it, but that the action of reading seemed to calm her). I put a glass of water on her end table and made sure that the medical alert button that she wore around her neck was working properly. Then I muttered a silent prayer to fate and hurried out to the car.

Fifteen minutes later, she got up out of bed, fell to the floor, and somehow managed to push the medical alert button. Within five minutes, our neighbor had let herself in with a spare key, but there was no way she was going to be able to lift Georgia by herself. So, the two of them sat on the floor in Georgia's bedroom for an hour, and that's where I found them.

It had been a year since we'd become a family of four, and it felt like the walls of our cozy little house on the corner were closing in on us.

Our teaching hours were adjusted so we were never away from home at the same time. We were cast in separate productions, so we'd never be rehearsing together. We barely saw each other day after day, except for the few minutes we spent at our changing of the guard at home. We were way over our heads, but we kept swimming in a fathomless current of our own making. I was too busy and duty-bound to stop paddling and notice that I was drowning.

Toward the middle of our second year in a state of siege, I took Georgia to her monthly checkup. Our own primary physician had assumed the routine of overseeing her care. I felt comfortable with Bruce because his daughter went to preschool with Sam, and they had become friends.

The checkup began like all the others: Bruce bounding his six-foot seven-inch frame into the room, the two of us catching up on Sam and Rachel's adventures at school; Bruce scooping the stethoscope off the base of his neck, a gesture that he performed in the assured manner of a guy who's been doing this for at least twenty years, and then placing the bobs in his ears and listening to Georgia's heart.

After taking her blood pressure, Bruce asked me to step out into the hall with him. I followed him into his office, bracing myself for whatever it was that he saw with Georgia that was worrying him. He sat on the edge of his desk and folded his long arms against his chest, and I watched his affable smile fade, as deep concern filled his eyes as he stared at me.

He was looking right through my protective mask, and the silence was making me squirm.

"Is she OK?" I asked.

"She's as well as we can expect. How are you?"

"A little strung out, I guess. This is harder than I thought."

He took a small pad of paper from his shirt pocket, jotted down something with a pen, tore the paper off the pad, and handed the sheet to me.

"This is somebody I think you should see," he said, pointing to the paper in my hand.

I suddenly felt unsteady on my feet.

"This is for you. I think you need to talk to somebody. I'll give him a call and see if he can fit you in."

He's sending me to a shrink. I don't need a shrink.

As I struggled through the thirty-minute process that involved walking Georgia to the car, helping her into the front seat, strapping her into the seat belt, and folding up her wheelchair and loading it into the hatchback, I let the guilt gremlins invade my thoughts. What is my problem? Why do I need a psychiatrist to help me through the scant sacrifices I'm making to take care of my mother-in-law? What kind of wimp am I?

Back home. Take Georgia out of the car. Wheel her to the side door. Transfer her to the walker. Help her falter inside. Get her settled in the overstuffed chair.

The light on the answering machine was flashing. I listened to the message.

"Jon and Gale, this is Dr. Reinhardt. Bruce called me and we discussed your situation. I've got an opening this afternoon. How fast can you get here?"

Chapter 41

O, I HAVE TA'EN TOO LITTLE CARE OF THIS

THERE WAS A SILENCE. Gale and I had been talking nonstop for forty-five minutes, and Dr. Reinhardt let the quiet in the room settle over us. Then he spoke, calmly but firmly.

"Today is Wednesday. I'm going to give you the name of a very good board and care facility close to where you live. I want you to call them. I want you to place your mother in this facility. And then I want you to come back on Friday and tell me you've done it."

I looked at Gale, seated next to me on the couch. She was silent, and I saw her looking to me for something. Did she want me to object? To agree?

"You have to think about what's good for Georgia," Dr. Reinhardt continued. "Your sense of duty is commendable, but it's not helping her. In fact, if you keep following what you think is your conscience, you will be hurting her. She needs constant care, and you are not going to be able to provide it."

Dan Quayle was right.

A space opened deep down in my chest. Was I filling that space with regret? Or relief? Tears were welling up inside me, and I buried them where I hoped Dr. Reinhardt couldn't see them.

"You may think you're alone, and that you're all she has. But she has doctors and nurses who can help her. You are not enough."

By Friday, as promised, we'd moved Georgia to the board and care, a five-minute drive from our house. I quickly fell into a routine every morning, dropping by to give Georgia her medications. Our life became manageable again. We even went back to the beach.

One afternoon, we were taking a long walk along the shore. Sam was running crisscross patterns around us. A slight breeze filled my head with the smell of seaweed and sand. The ocean lapped over my toes.

"Let's have another baby," I said.

Round-the-clock care for Georgia had ruled out the idea in my mind. But being surrounded by a sea of siblings my whole life, I wanted Sam to have at least one companion in life. Gale didn't object. After all, we had the Perfect Kid; who's to say that we couldn't have two?

Within the year, Emily entered our lives. We stepped on the accelerator and time flew by. There were days when the responsibilities I'd taken on were daunting. So many people were depending on me, acting students and my colleagues and family. What would happen if I got sick and couldn't function? Who would take my classes? Who would go on for me in the play that I was in? How are we ever going to get through the next two weeks before payday? When was I going to start learning lines for the *next* play?

It's a good life. It's a full life. But today it's so full that I think my head is going to explode.

Morning in Santa Maria was my favorite time of day. The fog would burn out by nine or ten, revealing yet another picture-perfect Chamber of Commerce don't-you-wish-you-lived-here Central Coast Day. The best part of it was that I *did* live here. The mornings always reminded me to treasure my days in Happy Valley. One day I'd be living once again amid snow and ice, but for now I was here, where it never got below 47 degrees and rarely above 80.

Each morning I'd drink my half-pot of coffee, pack the stroller full of diapers, baby wipes, and bottles of spring water, and set out with Emily, she of the brown shoe-button eyes and the pedestrian-stopping smile. She was already well known on our quiet tree-lined street full of adobe-covered bungalows and carefully tended gardens of fuchsia, roses, and the occasional bird of paradise.

One day Sam, now seven, walked by my side, dressed in his first grade best: lilac short-sleeve shirt buttoned at the neck and baseball cap pulled down over his eyes, the bill resting on his brows, shielding him from the sun and the scrutiny of strangers because that's how he was getting through first grade: by presenting himself as casual but reserved.

We were passing through the shade of the miraculous avocado trees. Once every other year they dropped luscious fruit in our backyard before inexplicably ceasing production. Those trees were their own reminders for me to appreciate the abundant times and be patient when life seemed to fall fallow. The canopy of leaves cooled me off as we crunched through downed acorns. But as we strolled beyond the trees and found ourselves in bright sun again, a spot at the tip of my spine was pricking at my dry skin. Soon a coil of itching was making me tingle, and I pulled off my windbreaker and contorted myself like I had St. Vitus' dance, vainly reaching with my fingers to scratch the most prickling spots. I let the stroller roll to a stop and Sam waited patiently for me to get the caravan moving again.

There was so much to see, and know, and savor. But on this morning my mind was rattling with a cacophony of unwelcome thoughts, drowning out the peace like a souped-up Chevy with a blasted-out stereo system scrambling the quiet of a summer night.

I looked down at Sam, at this wonderful kid growing up right in front of me. How did he get to be so tall that he stood even with my ribcage? Yesterday it seemed that he was no higher than my waist. How did I miss this? What else have I missed?

A bevy of house finches, sequestered in the trees, warbled an airy song and challenged me to stop for a minute and listen. Just listen.

At the end of the block stood the preschool that Sam had attended just two years ago, and where I had put in my eight hours a week as a participating parent. A line of four-year-olds, all holding hands, were in the crosswalk, on their way into the building. They were led by their teacher, Lola, the heart and soul of the school. From my vantage point of almost a block away, I could still see her fluffy crown of white hair, and her tender, loving smile. I'd spent two years at her school as a volunteer, and she'd inspired me every day in ways that made me not only a better dad, but a better teacher of acting. She'd changed my life, and I couldn't wait to return in two years, when Emily would be her student.

The kids' gleeful laughs danced along in the morning breeze. I stood on the sidewalk and closed my eyes. And for a moment I was back there.

Sam was four years old again, playing somewhere in this happy menagerie. But I couldn't stop to look for him. I had my job to do. Today was my day to clean out Snuggles's pen. Snuggles was a goat. He sniffed at my pants leg, jumping up at me, his cloven hooves digging into my denim-covered thigh. He was hungry. His water dish was empty.

Little poop pellets, dropped at frequent intervals, lined the pen. I was trying to rake them into a small pile, but Snuggles wanted to play. I looked around in the yard, at the kids on three-wheelers rollicking along the cement course; at the kids with water pitchers, anointing the plants; at the dramatic play corral, where one child after another flung open the half-door, rifled through the storage hampers, and pulled out costumes, each kid slamming the door before bounding up the ramp and into the classroom.

In about two hours I'd be dressed in a gauzy, mud-spattered tunic, soaked to the skin, struggling in vain to keep King Lear safe in his mad agony on the heath, a witness and celebrant in one of the greatest plays ever written. But first: Snuggles. I was toe-deep in goat poop, and this scrawny goat and a yard full of kids were counting on me to be present. Shakespeare would have to wait.

"Daddy?" It was Sam, gently tapping me on my ribcage, and bringing me out of my reverie back to the present. He had a concerned look on his face. I was still looking down to the end of the block at the preschool, but the kids had gone inside. I looked down at the stroller and saw that Emily was starting to stir from her nap. We still had a block to go to get to Sam's school. The bell would be ringing in a few minutes.

There was a breeze gently stirring the pine trees across the street, and the finches were joined by a few blackbirds singing me to attention.

My head cleared. My momentary visit back to preschool had rescued me from anxious thoughts that didn't belong and would do me no good. I placed my hands back on the handle of the stroller, and Sam and Emily and I rambled on toward school.

Rules for Actors, Rule #13: The key to good acting is also the hardest task: to live in the moment.

Chapter 42

WATCHING A PLAY WITH RAY

AT MY NEXT CONTRACT session with the management, my boss put down his pencil, stroked his beard nervously and asked me, "Would you be interested in directing something next year?"

This was a surprise. I had directed several plays in years past, but I hadn't been asked in a while and regretted that I'd been cut from the team without an explanation. I'd really enjoyed directing, and I missed it.

"What's the play?" I asked.

"*Dandelion Wine*, by Ray Bradbury. Do you know it?"

I lived on a steady diet of Ray Bradbury. I'd read all his novels when I was in high school, and one of my favorite story-theater experiences in St. Louis was narrating the entirety of his delectably apocalyptic tale, "There Will Come Soft Rains."

"I thought maybe a guy from the Midwest might enjoy working on it," offered my boss.

"Yes! Yes! I'd love to!" I bubbled, trying and failing to sound as if this was just another assignment.

The story is set dead-square in Bradbury's idealized Illinois. Most of it takes place outside in humid summer evenings, where cicadas and crickets dance in the deep grass. It's all musty smells, midafternoon showers, and moonlit nights.

It seemed as if the entire design team was composed of exiled Midwesterners. The set was a gently billowing sward of green in an emerald shade that I hadn't seen since I moved to California, and it featured a suitably scaled-down farmhouse front upstage, complete with a hanging swing on the porch. The sound designer contributed a stirring soundscape of crickets, robins, and buzzing bees that played quietly during the scenes when the boys bustled about capturing fireflies in the dusky evenings. I spent the happiest technical rehearsals of my life, two glorious days, listening to the sounds of the summers of my youth, seeing the sun come up and go down, and listening to a glorious score by a brilliant composer, Larry Delinger, himself a transplanted Nebraskan. As much as I loved the yearlong sunshine and mild temperatures outside the building, I reveled in the midwestern fantasy that our theater magicians had created onstage.

But as I studied the play, it was clear to me that this adaptation of the novel for the stage had some problems. The scenes were laid out in a sequence that I thought kept the story from flowing as smoothly as it could. So, I did some minor surgery, which I had no business implementing on a published script. I made improvements, and I assured myself that nobody would be sitting in the audience with a copy of the script, making sure I was not monkeying around with it. I cut a few lines I thought were expendable, moved some scenes around a little, and added a little group singing here and there. Who would know?

One day, a letter addressed to me arrived in the company mailbox.

Dear Mr. Daly:

I caught the article about your upcoming production of Dandelion Wine. I live right down the road in Santa Barbara, and I can't wait to come to Santa Maria and check it out. Let's get together beforehand.

Best, RAY

As in…Ray *Bradbury.*

My heart pounded. I hadn't met anybody this famous since Dana Andrews. And this was one of the greatest American writers of the century! In a county full of celebrities living in the Santa Ynez hills, Ray Bradbury was, in my mind, the king.

But you've messed with his play. The production has opened. You can't go back into rehearsal and get rid of all your changes. What if he sues?

On the day that he arranged to attend the show, I got a phone call from his secretary: "Mr. Bradbury would be delighted if you'd meet him outside the theater a half hour before the curtain."

I stood at the curb that night and watched as a limousine pulled up. The back door swung open, and I heard a booming voice: "Hello there, are you Mr. Daly? Hail, Maestro Director! Take a load off your feet."

I stepped into the car and flopped awkwardly on the backseat.

My God, it's a limo! I've never been in a limo!

There he was, in the flesh, extending a king-size paw. My hand disappeared into his. He shook it confidently, genially. He had a big, toothy smile, and his resonant voice seemed to rattle the windows.

Ray reached into a mini refrigerator at his feet and pulled out a bottle of champagne. He poured me a glass and raised his for a toast. "This is what's great about having Monty here drive me. I can have all the bubbly I want. And it's such a beautiful ride through the mountains. It's a little faster to fly up here, but I hate to fly."

Ray Bradbury hates to fly. You wrote The Martian Chronicles!!

We finished our champagne and left the comfort and safety of the limousine. As we crossed through the parking lot and approached the lobby, he loosely rested his arm in mine. "These old pins of mine aren't quite as steady as they used to be," he confessed.

When the house manager handed both tickets to me, I looked at our seat assignments. I was seated right next to Ray. I wouldn't be able to sneak out up the aisle when a sound cue was late, or a line was bobbled badly. I was stuck.

The first instance of my text tinkering came about twenty minutes into the first act. My shoulders tensed. I had to remind myself not to hold my breath. It wouldn't solve anything to pass out in my seat before intermission. When the action in the play shifted over to stage right, I took the opportunity to steal a glance in Ray's direction.

He's smiling.

The lights came up at intermission. Ray put his hand on my arm and flashed a sunny smile. "So far so good, Maestro."

I caught my breath. My spine unwound a little bit. But the biggest changes I'd made came in act two, where I inserted a song performed by most of the ensemble. I'd cribbed a few phrases of narration from the novel, and then I underscored the words with music: "I'll Be Loving You Always."

The second half started. This was it. He might hate this. He'd probably wait until after the show to call his lawyer.

The scene ended. As the lights shifted and the stage set for the next scene, the burly hand found its way to my arm. "I love that song. It's one of my favorites," Ray murmured. My grin expanded to fill the space between my burning ears.

Curtain call. The response was warm and full. The lead actor, my good friend Rick, took a step downstage, raised his hand, and spoke.

"Ladies and gentlemen, we have somebody very special in the audience tonight. He's agreed to visit with us for a few minutes if you'd like to stick around. Mr. Ray Bradbury."

There was an audible retort of surprise and delight. Ray rose slowly and waved to the good folks. I took his arm and led him down the steep steps to the stage. A comfortable rocking chair was fetched from the set. Ray stood at the chair, waving merrily, clearly grateful for the surge of applause. He unbuttoned his blue blazer, smoothed his striped tie over his yellow button-down shirt, and eased into the chair, adjusting the crease in his khaki pants.

He's still smiling.

Ray was the picture of graciousness that night. He took questions from the audience for a full half hour. They asked him about the play, and his other novels, and even the movies that were adapted from his work. When he was finished, he invited anybody who wanted to meet him to step onto the stage and say hello. He signed autographs for another half hour.

When the theater was finally cleared out, he turned to me and said, "How about a nightcap? I've got some more champagne chilling in the car."

In a few minutes I was back in Ray's limo, my tie loosened, sipping on the tastiest glass of champagne I'd had since my wedding day. Ray gleefully ticked off his favorite moments from the play, tossing superlatives into the air like little clouds of cotton candy. Never once did he challenge any of the changes I'd made. Had he even noticed them?

A week later, another letter from Santa Barbara found its way into my mailbox at work. It was from Ray.

Thanks for bringing my story to your stage. I can't think of a single thing that would make it better. Bravo, Director Extraordinaire!

Love, Ray

As I carefully folded the letter and pressed it into my autographed paperback copy of *Dandelion Wine*, I thought about how exciting it was to have my talent recognized by somebody as famous as Ray Bradbury. As much as I claimed to be perfectly satisfied to be a relatively anonymous theater worker, I could be as starstruck as the guy who waits in line for hours at a celebrity signing. And yet, living less than three hours away from Hollywood, the town where thousands of hopefuls flock every year hoping to find fame and fortune, I hadn't the slightest bit of serious interest in joining them. Fate commemorated the milestone of my fortieth birthday with a frank message: I was never going to be as famous as Ray Bradbury, or Dana Andrews, or any other notables with whom I might rub shoulders in future years. And for the first time in my life, I was content with that truth.

Chapter 43

THE DALY NEWS

SO NOW I WAS a director. Maybe it was time to become a writer as well, to finally write that play that I'd been thinking about for ten years, ever since I'd read our three-volume family history, *The Daly News*.

Back in 1991, the United States had fought in the Gulf War. Young men and women enlisted and were shipped overseas to fight.

That year I had taken Sam, at his insistence, to get his first official haircut. As I looked at his downy curls gathering on the floor, it occurred to me that one day he too would be eighteen.

What if we were at war in 2004? How would I handle it if they sent my son off to fight?

My grandfather had watched *four* sons go off to war. Now that I was a father, I had context for telling Martin Daly's story.

I started writing it as a solo piece, with me playing my grandfather, and the text adapted from Martin's letters to his kids. But I was holding something back. This was my story too, and I wanted to find my place in it.

At forty, I was still trying to come to grips with the distance I'd felt from my dad for our whole life together. Sam had given me the chance to redefine for myself what a dad can be for his son. And Martin, my grandfather, was a model I could count on to show me the way.

As I worked my way through Martin's letters, his words, intended as his effort to stay connected to his children, became my own private conversation with the grandfather who died seven years before I was born. What I had begun as a tribute to him became a memoir of my own journey to parenthood. And Martin gave me an unexpected gift—a snapshot of my own dad as a young man: dutiful, responsible, a little lonely, and enduring the pressure of being the oldest child. I was getting to know the father who had kept me at a distance, in a story told by the grandfather I never met.

By the time I was halfway through the first draft, I got the idea that the story would be best served as a musical. All the songs were inspired by my adolescent love of the big bands, the music I had used to try in vain to close the distance from my dad. I teamed up with two talented musicians and composers, Larry Delinger and Gregg Coffin. I wrote the book and lyrics, and they composed and arranged the extraordinary score.

I wrote most of the early drafts of the play between midnight and three in the morning. For the first two hours, I composed the text on a word processor. For the last hour, I moved the machine out to the garage, ran an extension cord from the inside of the house, and closed the three doors that separated the garage from our bedrooms so the sound would be muffled. I printed up page after page, hoping that the whining, clattering din wouldn't wake up everybody. This regimen kept me from getting any more than four or five hours of sleep a night for almost a year.

Gradually, the characters in the play emerged. There was Martin at the forefront, and his wife, my grandmother; my dad; his three brothers, and their wives, including my mom. Their songs almost wrote themselves because I took the lyrics from their own letters. There was my dad, singing about the pain of being away from his wife and newborn daughter; his siblings, chronicling the terror of a South Seas air raid, the boredom of Panamanian duty, and the one kid left at home, in a tongue-in-cheek boogie-woogie about the privations of rationing. The highlight of the first act was an Andrews Sisters-inspired threesome of GI wives wailing in close-order harmony.

I played the dual role of my grandfather and myself. After six months of drafts and rewrites, I found moments in the play when I'd remove Martin's wire-rimmed glasses and cozy cardigan sweater and literally inject myself into the story, speaking and singing directly to the audience.

Playing Martin *and* myself brought the play to life. Writing *The Daly News* led me to see my father through the eyes of *his* father. The play became the means by which I confronted and resolved the complicated ambivalent feelings about my dad that I had carried around since his death.

By the summer of 1993, the play was ready to go into rehearsals for a fall opening. I fretted that nobody would be interested in the story of a family living through an experience that thousands of others had had in 1940s America. But the colleagues and friends to whom I turned for support assured me that its universality was the very element that was going to touch an audience.

That summer, Gale and I were acting in a farce called *Lend Me a Tenor*, in which I played an unhappily married, temperamental opera singer named Tito Morelli, who had a madcap fondness for wine, whiskey, and barbiturates. You wouldn't think that a six-year-old would be entranced by such a spectacle, but Sam was no ordinary six-year-old, and his parents were up there making faces and getting cheap laughs. He must have seen it a dozen times, always sitting in the front row. God knows what the adults sitting around him were thinking. They were probably rendering private judgment on the permissive parents who would let their kid see such a bawdy, naughty farce with women running around in their underwear and the leading character popping pills.

At one point the script called for Tito to tear around the stage in a comically jealous rage before collapsing onto a sofa, where he slept for the rest of the act. We had a matinee one day, after I'd been up half the previous night, doing rewrites on *The Daly News* and fretting about whether my play was any good. I was exhausted and stressed out. I threw myself on the loveseat and prepared to spend the next quarter hour under hot stage lights, hoping that I wouldn't suffer the actor's nightmare of falling asleep and snoring in the middle of a scene. The laughter from the audience sounded to me like it was coming from the bottom of a swimming pool. The dialogue onstage began to distort, and the sounds of the play faded as if somebody had turned down the volume. I was losing the battle to stay awake, and the other actors weren't even halfway through the scene.

While trying to stave off unconsciousness but not draw any attention to myself, I pried my eyes open just enough to see cloudy colors. And there, standing at the foot of the loveseat, was my grandfather.

Martin wore the blue double-breasted suit that I'd seen in countless photographs from fifty years ago. He'd been dead for forty years, but there he was, looking at me with peaceful eyes framed by his familiar wire-rims, smiling gently. The stage lights made his white hair glow. He slowly raised his hand and gave me a genial wave, and then he was gone.

Everything was going to be OK.

And it was.

The Daly News: A Musical Memoir succeeded far beyond what I'd expected. My entire family flew out to see it: my siblings, my surviving uncles who were the original recipients of Martin's letters, and my mom, who set the whole labor of love in motion by printing up the three volumes in the first place.

The only one who missed it was the man for whom I hoped it would have meant the most: my dad.

Chapter 44

GREAT EXPECTATIONS

MARTIN DALY'S VISIT FROM beyond the grave wasn't the only watershed moment that marked *Lend Me a Tenor*. It marked the beginning of the end of Gale's career as an actor.

(Middle of the night. Bedroom. JON wakes up to find GALE sitting on the edge of the bed.)

JON

How long have you been awake?

GALE

I don't know…an hour or two, I guess.

JON

What's the matter?

GALE

I was standing backstage tonight, listening for my cue to go on, and all I could think of was, "I don't want to go through this door. I don't want to enter this world."

JON

I know you don't like the play very much.

GALE

It's more than that.

JON

Remember *Nicholas Nickleby?* We'd spend hours at the kitchen table, you picking apart every moment, fretting about how bad you were, and then the next day you'd show up at rehearsal and you'd be fine. It's the way you work.

GALE

It's the way I *live*. And it's hurting me. I've always tried to stay positive. To find my light and live in it. Our boy is out there every night, watching us. I do it for him. And for us.

JON

We're a team.

GALE

I don't know how much longer I can do this.

JON

It's what you love.

GALE

If I loved it, it wouldn't hurt so much.

(JON kisses GALE and turns out the light. He sleeps.)

AN OPPORTUNITY CAME HER way to adapt Dickens's *Great Expectations* into a play. Then she insisted on directing it. The production was stunning. Muscular. In fact, brilliant. She attacked the whole project with an energy and ferocity that shocked me, it was that good.

But the word came down from management. She was an actor, and if she wanted to keep her job, she'd have to act.

(Same bedroom, six months later. JON has been home for a month with the kids while GALE has been rehearsing Death of a Salesman. *He wakes to find GALE at the edge of the bed.)*

JON

What's wrong?

GALE

We ran through the play tonight. This wonderful play. All night I kept telling myself: just say the words, play the scenes, do what the script tells you to do. Tell the story. But we got to the last scene when Linda's kneeling at Willy's grave. Just say the line, I said. Just say the line. And I told Willy, "We're free, we're free," and I started crying. Sobbing. And I couldn't stop. Rehearsal was over, I got in the car, I drove home. And I'm still crying. I can't do this anymore. I just can't. It hurts too much.

(JON turns out the light. Nobody sleeps.)

SHE WAS SUPPOSED TO play the lead role in a Noel Coward comedy next. The part was perfect for her, they said. It was the kind of role that I thought she'd always loved to do.

But now she hated the very idea of it.

We started arguing more. Everything I said to console her seemed to aggravate her. I wasn't helping her. I was running out of platitudes, and I was losing hope that I could fix things. As every day went by, the temperature within our four walls was rising. If I took the trouble to look at the wallpaper, I could have seen that it was blistering.

And then a phone call from Milwaukee Rep. It was the offer I'd been waiting for my whole life. It was only one show, *A Christmas Carol*, but it was a start, and a chance to work in my hometown, at the very theater where I'd found my vocation in life.

I didn't hesitate, not for a minute. I'd never been so excited to accept a job.

I hung up the phone and danced around the kitchen.

Then came a thought that hit me with such force that I plopped with a thud at the kitchen table.

I was living in a house that felt like it was about to go up in flames. What was the point of escaping when my wife and kids were trapped inside?

Chapter 45

HAPPINESS TAKES HIS LEAVE

OUR TWELFTH ANNIVERSARY FELL two days before I left town. I planned a special gesture, not just a bunch of flowers or a box of candy. I'd spent a month learning and practicing one of her favorite arias, "Dein ist mein ganzes Herz," from the operetta *The Land of Smiles*.

When the day arrived, I met her outside of her classroom and held her hand as we walked into one of the rehearsal halls. My friend Brad was sitting at the piano. He'd lit a candle, and a red glow illuminated the room. All the other lights were dimmed. I sat Gale down at one end of the room and joined Brad at the piano. My knees were shaking. My breathing was shallow. I'd never be able to sing this thing without breath. I chugged a few gulps of water, took a deep breath, and started singing.

I hadn't sung three bars before Gale, recognizing the tune, began to cry. I was climbing the ladder of notes, a cliff of jagged rocks to the climax of the aria, and her cries echoed through the room. Wailing, anguished weeping.

I kept singing, determined to get to the end. With every note I was wrenching her heart, torturing her with this aria. When it was finally over, I rushed to her side. I quickly pulled up a chair and she buried her head in my chest.

How can I leave?

But I did.

Gale threw herself into yet another directing assignment while I was gone. *Julius Caesar*. Again, the same inexhaustible vigor, like she was on fire with a new creative ambition. She didn't miss being onstage at all. And she didn't want to go back.

Meanwhile, I was set adrift in my hometown, taking walks every morning, bundled up against cold weather for the first time in a decade. I was rehearsing for about five hours a day. It was a vacation after the schedule I'd been locked into for a decade. I spent a lot of my free time secluded in my vest-pocket-sized apartment. Every evening ended with a tearful phone call, racked with silent helplessness and guilt.

Was *this* what we wanted?

The Pabst Theater, where *A Christmas Carol* had been running every year since 1976, has been referred to as the Grande Olde Lady. It's one of the oldest theaters in Wisconsin, built in 1895. It's a proscenium-stage house, a drum-shaped jewel box of red and maroon. Gold leaf decor everywhere. Two full balconies, and the nosebleed seats at the top are the original stiff-backed, uncomfortable steel frames adorned with plush red-velvet cushions to ease the pain. If you sit in the front row of the top balcony, the angle at which the row leans toward the stage is so steep that it feels like if you aren't careful, you just might roll right over the brass railing and land in the orchestra. At the top of the drum is a two-ton crystal chandelier hanging from the ceiling. Audiences stroll through a grand lobby glistening with Italianate marble. It's the most elegant workplace around.

On the day that *A Christmas Carol* moved into the Pabst, I walked in through the stage door and saw that I was in the wings, mere feet away from the stage. I'd only been in the building once before, in 1976, when the Rep had first produced the play. Back then, the production marked the saving of the Pabst from possible demolition after it had been allowed to fall into a state of disrepair in the 1960s.

Soon, I was standing onstage with all the other actors, listening to the safety and orientation speech by the technical director. I didn't hear much of it because I was gawking at the grandeur all around me. The

Austrian crystal in the chandelier gleamed in the glow of the work lights. I could see into the side loges trimmed in red velvet and I imagined the occupants who sat there a hundred years ago. At one time, Laurence Olivier had stood where I was standing, as well as Katharine Hepburn, Alfred Lunt, Lynn Fontanne, and dozens of other theater greats.

The production turned out to be everything I hoped it would be. A first-rate acting company, glorious sets and costumes, and an enthusiastic audience every night filling the Pabst to capacity. In the twenty years of its run, *A Christmas Carol* had become a highlight of the holidays, and I was thrilled to be a part of it.

Enjoy this while you can. It's gonna end.

Meanwhile, Gale finished *Julius Caesar*, and the conservatory closed for winter vacation. The Noel Coward play and a return to acting loomed, but first there was Christmas. She and the kids flew to Milwaukee, and I met them at the airport. My heart leapt at the sight of Sam sprinting down the arrival gate, Gale following with Emily in her arms. We dissolved into a desperate tangle of arms and legs.

But that night I reached out for her in the bed, and she pushed me away. She sat up in bed and cried out, "I don't want to be with you anymore."

Chapter 46

"O, LET ME NOT BE MAD"

SHE DOESN'T MEAN IT. Everything's OK.

Christmas came and went in a hectic flurry of introducing the kids to snow for the first time and reacquainting them with their dozen cousins. I was with my mom and siblings for the first Christmas in five years, but I found it impossible to relax because I'd look at Gale and wince at her suffering. I wasn't sure what was wrong as I watched her plunge into blank, vacant stares, and her unexpected eruptions into agitation alarmed me even more.

I was relieved to go home. In a week, Gale was due to start the Coward play. Back to acting.

(January 26, 1996. Kitchen. JON is at the kitchen sink rinsing out a glass coffee carafe. He is nearing the end of a fourth consecutive day of manic housework. Painting the bathroom. Twice. Sanding and polishing the wooden floors. Moving the furniture. None of this is his idea.)

(The bedroom door opens for the first time all day. GALE is carrying a half-empty bowl of macaroni. She attempts to put the bowl in the sink. JON intercepts her, reaching out to take the bowl. GALE grabs

*his hand. JON pulls the bowl away. GALE pries the carafe out of
JON's other hand and pitches the carafe to the floor. Glass shatters
everywhere. She turns on her heels and rushes back to the bedroom,
slamming the door. JON can hear muffled crying through the walls
as he cleans up the broken glass.)*

*(Two days later. Evening. Living room. JON is paying bills. The
phone rings. JON answers it. It's TIM, one of the actors in the play
that GALE is about to begin.)*

JON
> Hey, Tim, what's up?

TIM
> Hi, Jon, is Gale there?

(A pause)

JON
> I think she's asleep. Can it wait until tomorrow? You'll see her at
> first rehearsal, right?

TIM
> Well…that's what I wanted to talk to her about.

JON
> *Oh no. Please don't say what I think you're going to say.*
> Tim, what is it?

TIM
> I've given it a lot of thought, Jon. I'm so sorry about this. But there
> are some things in my life that I've got to work out. I hate to do this,
> but I've decided not to do the show. I'm going to go home to my
> parents for a while.

JON

Tim, acting with you is the only thing that she's looking forward to about this play.

TIM

I've sensed that. That's why I wanted to tell her, so she wouldn't just walk into rehearsal tomorrow and not see me there.

(The door to the bedroom opens, and GALE appears. She stares at JON. She knows who he's talking to. She knows what's going on.)

GALE

Who is that?
It's Tim, isn't it?

JON

Yeah.

GALE

He's quitting, isn't he?

JON

I'll call you back, Tim.

(JON clicks off the phone. GALE closes her eyes. Her mouth quivers. She screams.)

GALE

NOOOOOOO!

(She pulls herself away and retreats to the bedroom, swinging open the door so violently that the doorknob punches a hole in the plaster. JON returns the phone to its cradle, as the sounds of violent sobbing fill the house.)

I RUSHED TO THE other side of the house, as Sam emerged from his bedroom. I couldn't hide my alarm, and I could see his.

No sooner did I get Sam to go back to his room than I heard Emily's voice.

I crept into her room. Her Winnie the Pooh lamp was on.

I picked up a book and laid down in the bed next to her. We read for a few minutes. Soon she was asleep. In a few minutes, my exhaustion caught up with me.

The next morning, I woke with the kids, we ate breakfast, I put Emily in the stroller, and we walked with Sam to school. When I got home, Gale was still in bed. As I put Emily in front of the TV, I noticed that the message light on our phone was blinking. I flicked the PLAY switch.

"Hi Gale, it's Judy. Did you forget you've got a costume fitting this morning? Give me a call."

I poured myself a cup of coffee. Then I tiptoed into the bedroom. The windows were wide open. The scent of jasmine and fuchsia filled the room. I bent down and touched her shoulder.

"Should I tell Judy to wait for you?" I asked.

A muffled, deliberate voice came from under the pillow. "I'm not going."

"Should I ask them to reschedule you?"

"I'm not going," she repeated.

"What should I tell them?"

"Tell them I quit."

My words caught in the back of my throat. I didn't have an answer to this. I couldn't fix it. I took a breath and gathered my thoughts.

"Do you want to call in sick?" I asked her.

She pulled herself up by the elbows to face me. Her face was pale, but her eyes burned with the feverishness of a woman who had either made up her mind or lost it entirely. Maybe both.

"No," she looked at me from miles away. "I told you. I quit."

Chapter 47

HOW DO I FIX THIS?

I CALLED OUR DOCTOR in a panic.

"Give me twenty minutes and I'll get back to you," he said, then hung up the phone.

Ten minutes later, he called back with the name of a psychiatrist who agreed to see Gale that afternoon. In less than two hours, we were sitting in Dr. Richardson's office. He asked Gale ten questions, and she answered yes to every one of them. Without skipping a beat, he diagnosed her as clinically depressed and possibly bipolar. My shoulders relaxed, as if he'd taken a fifty-pound weight out of my hands. She was sick, but her illness had a name. It could be fixed. Like a broken leg. Or a bad cold.

Two months went by. How naïve I'd been. This was just the beginning of a long road ahead. Stabilizing, stopping the emotional bleeding, beginning to rebuild synaptic bridges burned out by a lack of serotonin, these were all ideas that were new and perplexing to me. The pharmacological process of trial and error was unrelenting. One medication would work for a while, raising hopes that Gale would be improving, and then suddenly that medication would fail or have the opposite effect than was intended. Combinations of drugs would be tried, and they might interact disastrously with each other. Gale might spend hours seeing snakes slithering in the bedroom curtains, then be up moving the furniture or going on shopping sprees, then go to bed for days, barely able to function. The course of treatment, just to reach a state of balance, was hell on her.

And me.

My response to all the chaos, when I wasn't working or cooking meals or taking the kids to school or distracting them with trips to the park or the zoo or the grocery store or the car wash, *anything*, was to medicate myself. It started with a beer every night, then two, and sometimes three. After a few weeks of waking up with mild hangovers, I mentally slapped myself upside the head and quit cold turkey. What the hell was I doing? My job, as Gale reminded me, was to "carry the sanity ball." Our kids needed my presence, my patience, and my guidance. They were going to have to learn to live with Mommy's condition too, and it wouldn't help things any if I added a drinking problem to the mix. God, I hated giving up the beer buzz. But I had no choice. The imprint in my mind of my dad drinking himself into an early grave scared me straight. I had to learn other ways to deal with the stress.

(April 1996. A sun-filled, glassed-in office with a drop-dead view of the Santa Lucia Mountains. A stocky, clean-shaven man, dressed in tan blazer and matching slacks, is gently rolling a ball-point pen in the palm of his hand. His eyes are kind, his attention focused solely on his patient, GALE. She has been seeing DR. RICHARDSON several times a week for several months. Today, he's asked JON to sit in on the session, and after checking in with GALE, the doctor turns his attention to JON. When DR. RICHARDSON speaks, his manner is calm and unhurried.)

DR. RICHARDSON

Gale tells me that she may be going back to work soon.

JON

Yeah, they offered her a directing spot in the season. And she's got classes to teach too.

DR. RICHARDSON

But she's expected to be returning to acting, too.

JON

I guess they're hoping she'll be up for it eventually.

DR. RICHARDSON

Do you think she will?

(GALE is looking intently at JON.)

JON

I don't know.

DR. RICHARDSON

And how does that make you feel when you say that?

JON

Scared. And angry. I don't think anyone there cares how sick she is.

DR. RICHARDSON

Most people are uncomfortable with bipolar. Or depression. They're afraid it's contagious. It's not, of course. But it's affecting everybody in your household. Including you. You need professional help on your own. You need to talk about what you're experiencing, and most of the people you encounter on a regular basis don't understand what you're going through.

JON

People act like nothing's changed. Like there's nothing unusual going on. Sometimes I just want to grab people by the collar and yell in their faces.

(A long pause. DR. RICHARDSON waits. JON finally speaks up.)

JON

Yesterday we all had to line up to get our pictures taken for the summer program. Well, she didn't *want* to get her picture taken. I said, "Can't you just use the photo of her that you've used for the last five years?" "No, we're going for a nice uniform look."

This jerk lines her up against the wall. He says, "Oh come on, smile! You look so serious!" Then he says, "Come on! You're an actor! Just pretend you're a character in a play!"

DR. RICHARDSON

Can you see how hard that was for Gale?

JON

I wanted to slug the guy.

DR. RICHARDSON

Gale tells me you two have been acting together for a long time.

JON

We met acting in a play. We wanted to be the greatest acting team since Lunt and Fontanne.

(DR. RICHARDSON takes a moment, adjusts his silk tie, leans back in his chair. He looks at Gale, then once again turns his attention to JON.)

DR. RICHARDSON

I'm not an actor, obviously, but I think I have a pretty good idea what is required in your work. Emotional accessibility. Ability to reveal yourself in public. Moments of great stress and vulnerability. For Gale, living with bipolar disorder, acting is the worst profession she could choose. Even though she may be pretending that she's one of the characters she plays, her body and her mind can't tell the difference.

Gale tells me that you are quite an acting team. You've enjoyed working together over the years. Perhaps you are hoping that one day you'll be able to work together again. But I must tell you, Jon, that the dream you project is *your* dream, and not Gale's. I think she has known for some time that what she's doing is hurting her. But I'm not sure *you* know that.

MY BLOOD WAS RUSHING to my cheeks. My body felt bolted to the chair, afraid to move. My fingers turned cold, and somewhere deep in my chest a flame was flickering and fading. If Gale was going to recover and thrive, I had to accept that the dream, my dream, was over.

Chapter 48

CALL IT NOT PATIENCE, IT IS DESPAIR

(June 1996. The office of the artistic director. The building in which it resides, being the renovated site of a record-pressing plant, doesn't seem to ever have been intended as a place where humans gather to rehearse, conduct classes, and administer a professional theater.)

(Drywall, fluorescent lighting, and noisy ventilation ducts have rendered it a workspace, but the overall effect is that it's a sick building.)

(The artistic director never turns on the overhead fluorescent lights and has scattered various lamps around the room, giving the office the appearance of a dim dungeon. He has no internal control over the circulation of air, so the room is stuffy and stifling.)

(The artistic director, also known as the BOSS, sitting at a large oak desk, seems even more high-strung than usual, and his eyes are bouncing all over the room. His thin, reedy voice is quivering with nervousness. GALE and JON are taking this meeting together. There's a jittery tension in the room.)

BOSS

So, Gale…how's your mom doing?

GALE

She's been in the hospital all week. It's the second time in a month. She just can't keep anything down. I don't know if it's her heart, or her ulcers, or something else. I don't know how much longer she'll be able to stay where she is. She may be beyond semi-skilled care.

BOSS

I'm so sorry.

(There is an awkward pause while the BOSS tries to figure out how to change the subject. There's clearly no way to do it smoothly, so he dives into the reason for this meeting.)

I think we have some interesting things for both of you to work on next year. Gale, we've got another directing assignment for you. Jon, you've got a full season of acting work. And speaking of acting, Gale, do you think you'll be ready to go back on stage soon?

God Almighty, when are we gonna get beyond this? She's directed three plays, she's taught every class you've offered to her, she's even worked the souvenirs table in the damn lobby. What does it take for you to figure that out?

GALE

It's been a really difficult time for us lately. But not having to act has really helped—

BOSS

I know that. Really, I do. But for you to continue as an artist-in-residence here…well, I think we've made it clear…we need our artists to *act*.

(Silence)

JON

Let me make *this* clear. She's never going to act again. She can direct. She can teach. That's it.

(A chill overwhelms the room. The occasional door can be heard slamming down the hall. The BOSS stares blankly at some ill-defined spot somewhere over our heads. There is a silence. He swivels slowly in his chair and faces the wall.)

THREE DAYS LATER, GEORGIA was back in the hospital. Her vital signs were not good. Congestive heart failure. The attending physician warned us that she might not make it past the end of the month. He suggested that we arrange for transfer to a hospice.

On the same day that we moved Georgia to the hospice, we were called in for another meeting at the theater.

We walked into a room as cold as a meat locker.

Gale would direct one more play and then, because she refused to act in plays, she'd transition to a staff contract in the fall. Hourly pay. No health insurance. She'd be working for the college, but her position at the theater would be eliminated.

Her mother is dying, her health is hanging by a thread, and he's firing her.

Chapter 49

DEATH IS MY SON-IN-LAW, DEATH IS MY HEIR

WITHIN A FEW DAYS of her arrival at hospice, Georgia's vital signs were fading. Sometimes she was cogent and lucid; other times she seemed unaware of our presence. Her breathing was often labored. The nurses assured us that she was comfortable, but I looked at her swollen face, her mouth wide open, appearing to be gasping for breath, and I wasn't so sure. I looked around at her surroundings, at the semi-private room, at the dust gathering in the corners, at the plain white walls, and I hung my head, staring at the iron bed gate and sinking into a funk. I'd let her down. She didn't deserve for this to be the last place she took a breath.

On the morning of the first of July, 1997, Gale and I were with her. We stuffed all our angst into an imaginary balloon and let it sail into the clear blue sky. Gale held her mom's hand and told her she loved her. Georgia looked to Gale and mouthed, "I love you, too." For a moment, the snarled sound of her labored breathing stopped. I held my breath. Her mouth lay wide open, as if she was trying to seize air. It was the same shroud I'd seen on my dad's face on the morning he'd died. I waited, grasping Gale's free hand tightly. The silence in the room pulsed in my ears. I couldn't move.

Then Georgia's wheezing returned, and we stayed with her for a few more minutes. Eventually she settled into a brittle sleep. Gale kissed her mom on the forehead, and we stepped out of the room. We had meetings to go to, classes to teach. We'd visit her again at dinner.

The phone was ringing when we got home just before lunch. Georgia was gone.

We turned around and drove back to the hospital. The room where we'd been a half an hour ago was transformed. All the air seemed to have been sucked out of it. The beeping monitors stood silent. And Georgia, lying still under the covers, was no longer Georgia. Gale and I held each other. We didn't cry. We hardly moved. Our long struggle to give Georgia what we could was over. I was relieved and regretting that I felt that way. I looked at Gale, at the fathomless sadness in her eyes, and a somber loneliness settled in my bones. It was just the two of us taking on this grief; nobody else seemed to care.

Chapter 50

ALL'S CHEERLESS, DARK AND DEADLY

THE REST OF THE summer passed slowly. I found extra work teaching acting to apathetic adolescents who signed up for summer courses because they had nothing better to do. I taught theater appreciation to people who didn't. The assortment of minuscule paychecks added up to just enough for me to pay the mortgage, but I was falling behind on all the other bills.

I was angry. Resentful. But I clawed my way out of the darkness. I was determined to follow the light until it took me to where I wanted to be.

There were painful, difficult days. Even after I'd spent a month seeing a therapist two days a week, the coping skills I was developing didn't always see me through.

One afternoon, Gale was in the bedroom with the door closed and the kids were at school. I was in our cramped kitchen, gazing around at its fixtures, unchanged since the early sixties. Red Formica countertops. A linoleum floor in a red-and-white checked pattern. Wooden cupboards painted stark white from the manic home improvement of last year. I'd always enjoyed the shabby gentility of the room, but today it felt barren and hopelessly out of date.

I brushed aside the short peppermint curtains over the sink and stared out the open window to the street. The morning mist had burned out, revealing yet another picture-perfect day, contrasting with the dark clouds in my head. Ever since Gale's psychic break, I had been holding it together for the kids, for Gale, for me.

But now, my foundation was shaking like a wooden balance puzzle with its center piece pulled out. First came the tears. Then my breathing degenerated into spasms as I gasped for air. Then I couldn't stop the sobbing. I didn't care if the whole neighborhood heard me. My temples were throbbing, my jaw aching. This wasn't a purge or a healthy release. I was falling apart.

My therapist had been encouraging me, whenever I felt like I was losing my way, to grab an hour if I possibly could and get outside. Take a walk. Get some exercise. I grabbed the car keys, made a beeline for the car, and pointed it west. In half an hour I was trudging across the dunes, slipping and sliding in the deep sand. I reached the edge of the shore where the surface was firm and the gulls were scampering alongside me. On this day, like most days, it was warm enough for me to kick off my shoes and go wading in the ocean up to my knees. The sky was dappled with clouds, but there was plenty of sun beating down on my shoulders. The din from the roiling waves drowned out my turbulent thoughts. I stood in the waves, willing myself to take in as much sea and salt and wind as I could. I drank it all down in big gulps, pushing it all down my windpipe into my gut. I was hoarding as much energy and power as I could hold. I wanted to save it all, this life force of psychic reserve, squirreling away so much soothing grace for use on the rainy, dark days that suddenly seemed perilously close.

Nothing lasts forever.

I'd been telling myself that for years. It was one of those docile proverbs that was easy to say but difficult to absorb. When times were bad, the thought consoled me. When times were good, I pushed it out of my mind. But today all whimsy was slipping, like the surf receding in front of me. What was left behind on the shore was rock-solid, bold-printed certainty.

This will all be over soon. This cannot be sustained.

Over the next few weeks, I did all I could to hold on for as long as I could. I had to keep it together until I figured out what to do next.

I kept the mask that I wore at work firmly in place.

I acted in the plays that I was asked to be in. I took no joy from it, but at least I was paying some of the bills that had been accumulating. At least PG&E wasn't going to turn off our power.

The school year began, and our team of artists-in-residence assembled for the first meeting of the year. Gale's desk sat in the middle of the bowling-alley-sized office that we all shared. She hadn't been in to clear out her files and books, so her workspace loomed over the meeting like a metal grave. Nothing was said. All but one very kind colleague pretended that nothing had changed.

But there were surprises too. By the time I'd been through the first month of the school year, I noticed that I was enjoying teaching more than I had in years. I no longer cared about getting anyone's approval to keep my job, so it freed me to express myself in my work. Instead of dragging my feet into class every day hoping that I wouldn't fail, I strode into the room with confidence. The classroom projects I chose to work on excited me, and my students seemed to be responding with enthusiasm. They bounced into class every day ready to work. The material was full of sex and violence and blood and gore. All heightened text, all classical in nature, and they dove into it all with relish. If anybody looked closely, they would see that my choice of material revealed the anger that was consuming me, but the work was challenging and useful and FUN!

I forced myself to confine my worrying about the future to ten minutes per day. When ten minutes were up, I posted a guard at the door to my brain and refused to admit fretful thoughts. At first it felt stupid, but after a while, despair began to fade.

And then of course there were Sam and Emily, who kept me going. Above and beyond anything, I was a dad, and that part of my identity was creative, satisfying, and gratifying. Teaching Sam to ride his bike in the DMV lot, empty during off hours. Strolling down the shady lanes around our house with Emily. Stopping at the indoor mall and buying soft pretzels and watching Emily riding the miniature carousel round and round. No matter what fretful thought might be looming, I would be there to smile and wave every time she appeared.

One day in late fall, Sam and I drove out to the beach. The wind was bustling, tossing up sand in our faces as we ran. We pulled our baseball caps over our eyes, laughing as we lurched toward the shore.

I put my arm around Sam, and he leaned into me. Then he took my hand and we just stood looking out at the pounding waves.

It occurred to me that my coping mechanism of storing the sea in my solar plexus was no longer serving me. I wondered if it ever really had. I didn't need to hoard these surroundings anymore.

I took one last long moment to gaze out at my watery protector from the last dozen years, the roaring sea that I had counted on to stay sane, and a placid thought came to me.

I can say goodbye to this. I can come see it again sometime. But for now, I'm ready to let it go.

Rules for Actors, Rule #14: If the role no longer suits you, be ready to walk away.

Chapter 51

OPEN LOCKS, WHOEVER KNOCKS!

WHEN A DREAM FINALLY comes true, a dream you've been holding on to for years, it doesn't always quite play out the way you'd expected.

The phone call finally came from Milwaukee Rep. They offered me two shows and three months of work. For me, that was a long-term job. But as soon as I hung up, two competing trains of thought came steaming down the track, on parallel courses, their wails and whistles reaching my ears at the same time, vying for my attention.

This is everything I've ever wanted.

What the hell am I doing?

I was poised to uproot my family, dragging them to a town in which they'd never lived, leaving paradise behind, and subjecting them to snow and ice and subzero winters, as well as summers that seemed to come and go in a cruel flicker of time. It meant new schools, new doctors, new friends. For me it meant longer hours and farewell to the flexibility of a schedule to which I'd become accustomed. It meant working six nights a week with no exceptions, missing out on story time with the kids and the familiar rituals I'd been enjoying for the better part of a decade.

I stepped outside for some fresh air.

Sixty-seven degrees and a sky full of stars. Crickets and nightcrawlers stirring, the usual traffic noise from the main thoroughfare three blocks away, stolen by a mild westbound breeze. I could hear the soft sound of my own footsteps. The canopy formed by the pine trees barely stirred.

I was wearing a short-sleeved cotton shirt and shorts. I hadn't bothered to grab a coat or a sweater on my way out the door. Back in Milwaukee, it was probably raining. Maybe even snowing, grimy gray piles of slush piling up on the streets.

Not here. Never here.

I stood in our front yard, leaning on the twenty-foot-high redwood that stood right outside Sam's bedroom. His light was still on. He was probably getting in a little more reading before sleep.

Emily was already dozing because we had finished the nightly ritual some time ago. I'd carried her on my back and dumped her on the bed. I'd filled her purple plastic cup with water. She'd turned on her white-noise machine and signed out on the small chalkboard in her play kitchen, just like she did at the preschool. We'd recited our "God blesses"; we'd read our two stories; I'd wound up the musical orb and we'd sung our nightly lullaby, the one about a cow jumping over the moon.

I'd waited until she fell asleep, and then I'd snuck out of her room and wandered into the night.

Now, I was standing on the lawn made uneven by the redwood tree roots that lay just below the surface. The house was quiet. And I murmured to myself, my words breaking through the stillness of the night air: "How can I take them away from everything they know?"

I sauntered around the block. I would miss this. I couldn't imagine a quieter place anywhere in the world.

I was back in front of our house in a few hushed minutes, again standing next to the redwood tree. The trunk was so wide that when I would try to hug it, my hands didn't touch. Tonight, I didn't try.

(Next day. Back in the office of the artistic director. Somehow it doesn't seem nearly as gloomy or stifling as it usually is. The BOSS is leaning back in his chair, hands on the desk, smiling up at JON,

his eyes sharp and yet distant as ever. He is chipper and cheerful in a starched blue-denim shirt and ironed khakis.)

JON

I've got an offer in Milwaukee. I'm leaving at the end of the summer.

(The BOSS's eyes flood with tears)

BOSS

(Choking out the words)
Oh, what you've been through!

(The BOSS jumps out of his chair, darts around his desk, and throws his arms around JON, who waits out the awkward moment like a kid forced to hug an aunt he barely knows. The BOSS suddenly stops crying, as if a plug leading to his heart was pulled out of the wall.)

BOSS

That's just great! Great! How's Gale doing?

JON

You fired her. Don't you remember?
She's fine. Well…I have to go. I just wanted to tell you.

(JON exits. He stops at the bulletin board and tacks up his resignation announcement for the students and faculty. The stale recycled air floats through the ceiling vent. There is the usual hum and buzz of fluorescent lights. The posters on the walls of past productions look muted, their bright colors dimmed, as if they are already receding into the past. He rushes out the front door before seeing anyone. It's over.)

Chapter 52

I SEE YOU STAND LIKE GREYHOUNDS IN THE SLIPS

I PULLED OUT OF the parking lot and went straight home and started packing. Twenty boxes in the first two days. I began the long process of casting off what we didn't need to move halfway across the country. I packed every night till midnight and was up five hours later going at it again. I was *crazed*. It was as if I'd been stuck in a state of suspended animation for months, maybe years, and suddenly the mad scientist who had locked me in the Chamber of Insensibility had released me.

Within a week, I had painted four rooms and taken a dozen carloads of stuff to Goodwill. And I never felt tired, even when I fell into bed at night after having performed in a play for three hours.

And the role I was playing onstage was a drag. Really. A literal drag role.

One of my colleagues was directing a musical called *Once Upon a Mattress* and he asked me if I'd consider a really silly idea. Would I be willing to play Queen Aggravain?

Why not? I'll be out of here in four months. I might as well have some fun.

I donned an exquisitely designed gown and capered my way through this campy musical comedy playing the queen, in drag. The talented costume designer, a good friend who had clothed me as Cyrano and John Proctor, set me up with a rehearsal hoop skirt, an ample brassiere stuffed with ten pounds of bird seed, and a headdress that made me look like a swell-headed peacock.

I pranced around the rehearsal hall, singing in a falsetto and swinging my artificial boobs and butt from side to side. I was having too much fun to be fretting about paying bills, selling the house, and moving everything we owned in a U-Haul. The queen was a catharsis, an escape hatch, an unexpected joy.

The bonus came when the play opened and I heard the laughs of recognition from the audience, many of whom had seen me in almost fifty roles. I'd be leaving them soon, and the thought saddened me. They'd first seen me when I was a callow young character actor in my late twenties, and now I was well past forty. I'd be starting over in Milwaukee, and it might take a few years to build the same connection to an audience that I had in California. But the die was cast, and for the first time in a long time, it felt like I was moving on to bigger challenges.

By August, I was in rehearsal during the day for my last play, *Ten Little Indians*, an old chestnut of an Agatha Christie murder mystery, while sashaying as the queen in the evenings. Our house was stacked floor to ceiling with boxes, all ready to be packed into the truck. Our car would be loaded onto a flatbed trailer, and I'd be hauling the whole mess to our new home, two thousand miles away. Sam would ride with me in the front seat. Gale was all for the idea. I had packed up the house virtually by myself, and she was perfectly content to let me finish the job. For me, it was all part of the joyful transition to a new life and a bonding adventure with my boy. What could be better?

A week before we were due to start our trek, Gale and Emily were to fly on ahead nonstop to Milwaukee. We drove down to LAX, and Sam and I dropped off Gale and Emily at the terminal entrance. Then Sam and I wended our way through the maze of parking terminals, looking for a place to park the car.

(Forty-five minutes later. JON and SAM dash into the terminal, having sprinted the equivalent of two city blocks. DAD is soaked in sweat, fire in his eyes.)

JON

(Roaring to the hapless TICKET AGENT)
Where's my wife? Where's my daughter? Daly's the name. D-A—

TICKET AGENT

(Smiling, hoping to defuse the ticking bomb standing in front of him)
Sir, they've already boarded. We're right on time.

JON

(His voice climbing an octave)
But we didn't say goodbye. I couldn't find a parking space. We have to say goodbye.

TICKET AGENT

(Keeping his cool)
I'm sorry, sir, but we've already begun departure procedures. It's already too late.

JON

But if it hasn't taken off yet, why can't I just go out there and say goodbye to them?

TICKET AGENT

I'm sorry, sir, but we can't do that. The plane will be taxiing soon. You can go to the window and wave to them.

JON

(Out of control and now screaming)
But I want to say goodbye to them! Call the plane and tell them we want to say goodbye!

(The TICKET AGENT takes a moment to evaluate whether to call security and have this wild man Tasered in front of his son, or to resolve it peacefully. HE looks at the desperation in JON's eyes, maybe he imagines himself in a similar situation.)

TICKET AGENT

Sir, I can have your wife step out of the plane for a moment and meet you here.

(JON stands in the middle of the airport terminal and recovers his senses. He resists the impulse to get down on his knees and thank this wonderful, kind man.)

IN A FEW MOMENTS, Gale and Emily appeared from the hangar. I hugged them both with a grip that pushed them back against their heels. I was damp with sweat and tears. I kissed them goodbye, and they hurried back to their seats. Our escape from paradise was underway.

Chapter 53

HERE'S YOUR HAT, WHAT'S YOUR HURRY?

CLOSING NIGHT.

After thirteen years of performances, it was down to one more night. Three more hours. I had bid goodbye to Queen Aggravain the weekend before. The truck was packed. Our car was mounted on the flatbed. In the morning, Sam and I would drive away. At dusk, I walked Sam over to our friend's house just a few blocks away. I would join him there when I was done with the play. I set out for the walk to the theater, the same stroll that I'd taken hundreds of times. I allowed extra time so I could stop to gaze at every favorite house, every tall pine tree, every landmark that I'd taken for granted. Now all of it was precious, hosting an avalanche of memories. The pool where I'd taught my kids to swim. The preschool. The open field at the edge of campus where we'd flown kites. It was all in the past. Sam had spent the first ten years of his life here, Emily her first five. We were leaving a part of our lives behind.

Approaching the theater, I walked past the large boulder that had stood incongruously on the lawn for years, since long before we'd moved here. It had never occurred to me that its presence on the middle of a college campus was at all unusual. Over the years, it had served as a resting place, a meditative spot, and a great place to pose for pictures. We had photos of everybody in the family on this rock. Tonight, it had been transformed into almost a sacred site to me. I took one last look at it before I walked through the stage door.

In a delightful irony, I was performing a play in which a stage full of characters disappeared one by one, done in by a psychopath who kept his identity secret until the final scene. What made it unintentionally perfect was that *I was the murderer*. The final scene called for me to reveal my crimes, aiming a revolver at the surviving guests, and delivering an unhinged, embittered monologue. I couldn't think of a more fitting, poetic way to put an end to a tenure that had once been happy but had ended so painfully.

As I worked my way through the first scene, my focus splintered between performing the play as we'd rehearsed it, looking in the eyes of my fellow actors, being present for them, and drifting into memories of previous shows. I was standing on the stage in the same spot where I died as Cyrano. When I took a few steps upstage, I was where I'd held Gale's hand in *The Crucible* as I ascended the gallows as John Proctor. Another spot was where I'd sat at a table balancing a spoon on my nose in *The Foreigner*. And downstage center, Gale and I had danced in the closing moments of *Much Ado About Nothing*, when Georgia was so ill, and we had clung to each other for support. I was in all these worlds at once; and in a flash of time, we were doing the final scenes of *Ten Little Indians*, the clock running down, the moments passing as the lines of the play flowed through us and into memory. One of the most wondrously heartbreaking qualities of the theater—its fleeting existence—was playing out before my eyes..

I spoke the last line of the penultimate scene. The lights faded to black, and I turned around and began to walk toward the wings, just as I had every night for the last month. I looked for the dim backstage work light that would guide me to the quick-change station. I was under self-induced pressure to be speedy and direct. But everything just looked black to me. Pitch black. Not-being-able-to-see-your-hand-in-front-of-your-face black. I panicked. I swiveled slightly to one side, then to another, like a semi driving too fast on a rain-slicked highway. I couldn't see anything. I had only a few more seconds before the lights would come up on the next scene, and I wasn't supposed to be there.

I took a few tentative steps and felt the floor give way. It was only about an eight-inch drop, but it was as jarring as if I'd stepped off a high platform. I walked face-first into one of the permanent walls of the theater. I spun around and my shin slammed against the eight-inch riser. The force of the impact dropped me to my knees. I swung my arms forward to see if I could grasp anything that might lead me to figure out where I was. My right arm smashed into a standing lamp, and the whole thing landed on my arched back before crashing to the floor. I crawled around the lamp, hoping the bulb hadn't broken and scattered shards of glass in my path. The palms of my hands burned, and so did my knees. I thought my pants had torn, and my right knee felt like it was gushing blood. I saw a faint glimmer of light to my right and followed it desperately, once again sliding off the platform to the stage floor below. My forehead smashed into the floor, and I crawled miserably to safety.

A stagehand was waiting for me with my costume. I tore off my sweater and tie, put on its counterpart, straightened my glasses, brushed my hand through my hair. Sweat was pouring off my face. I looked down and noticed my pants weren't torn after all; the audience wouldn't have to endure the sight of blood running down my legs.

I made my entrance with seconds to spare, my panic belying the suave, cool, detached murderer I was supposed to be. And when I revealed myself to be the homicidal maniac, I had no problem acting unhinged. My knees were on fire, and I sped through my final speech, thinking only of getting off stage and icing my knees.

But first, I had to die. I pulled out my gun, and then the hero of the play put me out of my misery with a shot through the heart.

As I lay center stage and the lights faded to black, I tapped a light farewell to the stage with my knuckles and then bounded to my feet for the curtain call, a dead player come to life.

I smiled my way through the tepid applause and jogged off the stage. Once I got to the dressing rooms, I found myself hurrying to get away.

I'd really been leaving for several months, and I didn't want to spend a lot of time with sentimental goodbyes. There were a few people who wanted to wish me well, and I accepted the gestures with as much grace as I could summon.

As I reached the sidewalk that led to the back exit of the campus, a woman approached me. I recognized her from her rose-colored pantsuit and her shock of white hair. It was Lola, my mentor at my kids' preschool. Lola, who had guided me through the challenges of early parenthood. Lola, from whom I'd learned more about teaching and creativity than anyone else. I couldn't have imagined a better person to see me off on this night.

She wrapped me in a firm hug, then pulled away to look me in the eyes. She held on to my arms. I felt my haste melt away. She waited another moment and then spoke.

"I don't think I ever told you this before, Jon, but a few years ago my family was going through a rough patch. My mother had been sick, and my children were all grown and on their own. It was just very sad around our house. And one night I asked my mother if there was anything that she thought would be fun for us to do. She said, 'Let's go to the college and see a play.'

"It was that comedy show you did, with the actor you did *The Foreigner* with."

Oh God. That terrible play with the ridiculous title. Dopes on a Rope. *What a turkey.*

"Well, we saw it and laughed and laughed," Lola continued. "It brought us both out of our funk, and I swear it added a year to my mother's life. I never thanked you for it, but I'm grateful that I got the chance tonight. Safe travels, Jon. I'll miss you so much."

Lola was still teaching me.

Rules for Actors, Rule #15: Never disparage your own creative work, because you never know the difference it can make in somebody's life.

A last hug, a heartfelt goodbye, and I slipped away into the night. A sliver of a moon and a scattering of stars guided me on my walk.

My eyes were dry, but my heart was full.

Chapter 54

YOU *CAN* GO HOME AGAIN

THE APARTMENT THAT WAS to be our new home in Milwaukee was the bottom half of a sprawling 1920s duplex, four doors down from the house where my dad had grown up. I was living a few steps away from the house where my grandfather composed *The Daly News*.

Sam and I arrived on the hottest day of the year, with the humidity way over eighty percent. We clearly weren't in Central California anymore.

Gale and Emily were waiting for us, along with my siblings, their spouses, and my mom. After pining over this day for so many years, I was finally home. Gale smiled. She was happy too.

Mosquitoes feasted on us as we spent hours emptying the U-Haul and carrying our belongings over the threshold. My eighty-year-old mom was right in there with us, lending a hand whenever she could. When our bed was assembled, she unpacked the bedsheets and made the bed herself. "Always unpack your sheets first and make the bed right away," she'd been advising me since I was a college kid. "That way you can fall into bed at the end of the day without having to make a fuss."

When the truck had been emptied, I took a moment to look out of the bow windows lining the north wall. Spread out in front of me was a grassy boulevard lined with stately duplexes and bungalows, all of which looked like they had been standing there for almost a century. The neighborhood had hardly changed since my dad and his siblings roamed the sidewalks.

My whole family was gathered around me, and I had a sudden, rhapsodic thought, one I hadn't had since I'd become an adult twenty-five years ago. I was going to host Thanksgiving dinner this year, and I had a lot for which to be thankful.

The mountain of boxes had been cleared away by half by Labor Day. Now it was time for Sam and Emily to brave the first day of school. Sam had it tougher. He had left behind a class of forty kids housed in a couple of modules in an open field with emerald-green mountains in the distance, and he was now confined to a brick fortress that extended the length of a city block, containing two thousand kids bused in from all over the city. He was dropped into a world of locker inspections, guards in the hallways, and metal detectors, and his eyes filled with tears of panic as we listened to the principal lay down the law at the first assembly. It was the best public middle school in town, and it was on the track for the international baccalaureate high school; but it was loud and chaotic and scary.

After the principal's "scared straight" lecture, I took Sam by the arm, and we walked up to the front of the room. "Let's meet your principal," I assured him.

Sam had changed a lot in the last few months. It was almost as if he'd left his childhood behind in California. He'd had a growth spurt, and he'd taken to buttoning the top button on his shirts, as if he was trying to keep his worries sealed up inside. His Bermuda shorts had been replaced by long-legged khakis. He was preparing for colder weather, inside and out.

I introduced us to Dr. Hazzard, a towering bald-headed man with a pencil-thin beard along his jawline. He was dressed in a gray silk suit, and an elegant stick pin adorned his brightly colored tie. I greeted him earnestly and introduced Sam. Dr. Hazzard took Sam's quivering hand into his own, flashed a confident smile, and boomed, "I am very glad to meet you, Samuel. You are going to enjoy a shining success here. I can tell by looking at you."

I felt better as we walked to the car. I wasn't so sure about Sam.

Emily made no attempt to hide her fear. She cried the first full week of kindergarten. The combination of normal separation anxiety and being in an unfamiliar place was causing her serious distress.

And then it was time for *my* first day.

It was the hottest day of the summer. The bus downtown was late. I sprinted the last few blocks. I ducked into the slow-as-molasses elevator, exited at the fourth floor, and darted into the rehearsal hall. I was soaking wet and wheezing like an accordion.

There must have been a hundred people in the room, all gathered for welcoming speeches, design presentations, and the momentous first reading of the play. We introduced ourselves one by one. I'd been dreaming of this moment for years, so when it got to me, I stepped forward and waved as if I'd won a prize at the state fair.

The director of the play walked to the front of the room and began to speak. He launched into a passionate, eloquent presentation of how he was going to direct the play, what he thought were the important themes, and how excited he was to work with a brilliant group of actors. I was thrilled to be in the room and simultaneously filled with anxiety. I was in the big leagues now.

We barreled our way into the first week of rehearsals, taking more time at the table picking apart the play than I'd ever done. When it came time for me to read my small part, I was stiff and self-conscious, and I tried to quell the petulant voice inside me.

You stink. And look at all those actors looking at you. I bet they're trying to figure out how you got this job.

True, the actors did seem a little reserved as the days went on. But it wasn't because of anything *I* was doing. They were starting to figure out that this comedy was about as funny as an obituary.

I was simply happy to have the job. Complaining about the play seemed pointless and presumptuous of me. It was a fine line to observe. Ignoring its faults would result in allowing this fledging little pink pachyderm to grow into a full-sized elephant in the room; but too much criticism would foul the atmosphere and the actors would grow embittered. Either way pointed to failure, but our director did everything to mine gold from granite. He filled the stage with creative distractions, he encouraged the actors to make bold choices. But ultimately the play, well…

(1998. One week into the run of JON's first play at the Rep. Audience talkback. The director and cast are seated in chairs, sheepishly smiling at the few audience members who have stuck around.)

DIRECTOR
Yes, I see a hand in the back row. What's your question?

ANONYMOUS AUDIENCE MEMBER
What made you decide to do this play?

DIRECTOR
Well, there are a lot of considerations. We look for contrasts with the rest of our season, we look at cast size, we look at opportunities for our resident actors—

ANONYMOUS AUDIENCE MEMBER
No, I get all that. I just want to know. What made you decide to do…*this* dog?

(Talkback ends. As the audience departs, a woman is heard complaining to her companion.)

DISGRUNTLED WOMAN
For this we passed up *Cats*!

I'd left a so-so production of a good play in California to do a so-so production of a *stinker* in Milwaukee.

I didn't care.

It would get better. Right?

Chapter 55

GOD BLESS US, EVERYONE

I WAS IN MY first production of *A Christmas Carol* when I was twenty-five, donning a cock-a-hoop wig that made me look like a young Michael Caine and cavorting my way around the stage as one of Fred's Christmas party guests. I was also one of three narrators who began each performance in the lobby, singing madrigal carols skillfully arranged by the music director. It was the first play I had done on the Mainstage in St. Louis, and I loved every minute of it. I was also called on to understudy Scrooge. I never went on, so the audience was never forced to pin their sense of belief on the shoulders of a kid young enough to be their child.

Ten years later, I got to play Scrooge in California, but I was still much too young, and outside, the weather was sunny and incongruously warm. I was getting close, but not quite there.

Another decade passed and I'd made it to the Pabst, and I was understudying Scrooge again. By now I was old enough to be conceivable in the part, and when I was told I'd be going on for four performances at the end of the run, presumably to give the real Scrooge a much-needed rest amid a long run, I was thrilled.

I showed up for every minute of rehearsals, taking notes and watching the actor playing Scrooge as he prepared the role. He'd been doing it for years, but he was steadfast about re-examining every moment, never content to rely on what had worked in the past. As his character never left the stage, there were hundreds of little details that I wanted to learn.

I was spending ten hours a day with *A Christmas Carol*, rehearsing my own roles while learning Scrooge. It felt like I was in practice watching Mickey Mantle in center field, knowing that I'd be substituting for him during the last few innings of the game, after the team had clinched the victory. Over time it became clear to me that the management was watching me carefully, seeing whether I was up to the task of absorbing all the technical details while demonstrating potential for creating my own approach to the part. Scrooge was the flagship role in the Christmas franchise, and I had to earn my way into contention for it. Despite the pressure, I never felt anxious or overwhelmed.

I was ready.

I walked through the role on the last day of the weeklong period of technical rehearsals, when full performance conditions prevailed. Hundreds of lighting, sound, and scene-shifting cues were meticulously designed, executed, and rehearsed. The whole cast was in full costume and makeup. I had to be in the right place at the right time without fail. There was no room for approximating. I had to be in pinpoint-perfect position for the lighting and sound cues to work. A couple of inches too far forward or backward or off to the side could ruin the entire stage picture that the designers spent hours building. And with literally tons of scenery being raised and lowered by pulled force from the wings offstage, if I was off "spike," I was putting myself in lethal danger.

As the clock neared midnight, I was standing in a pin-spot of light while the designer adjusted the angle of the beam's direction to correctly frame a slightly taller Scrooge, and I looked out at the thirteen-hundred-seat house, knowing that in a few weeks every single seat would be filled, and they'd all be looking at ME. I was going to be filling the shoes of not only the current Scrooge but all the actors that came before him, including the actor I had seen on this very stage back in 1976, when I first dreamed of one day acting at Milwaukee Rep. The awareness that my dream was going to come true took my breath away for a moment and then filled me with a humbling, ardent joy. I stood alone center stage, bathed in light, and held the moment to my heart.

The next day, I settled back into playing Bob Cratchit, happy to be out of the spotlight for a while. And when my personal opening night came, I wasn't restless or anxious. Just quietly thrilled.

It was a suitably snowy evening when I got my chance with Scrooge.

I was sitting at Scrooge's spot in the upstairs dressing room, applying a sallow makeup base followed by carefully drawn shadows and highlights, donning the nylon skullcap cross-aligned with bobby pins to receive the shoulder-length wig soon to be fitted to my head. The audio monitors were on in the house, so I could hear the head usher giving his nightly instructions to his volunteers just before the audience was admitted.

From my perch three stories above the orchestra, I heard him say, "There's an understudy going on as Scrooge tonight, so I suppose anything could happen. I just hope he's half good."

You just wait, pal.

I walked out of the dressing room and stepped onto the iron platform, three stories above the stage. I had spent a month standing on the opposite platform, just outside the room I shared with the actor playing Jacob Marley, gazing down at the stage and watching Scrooge's every move whenever I was free. I'd learned exactly where he stood at every moment. I'd memorized his movement patterns as he skillfully avoided thousands of pounds of stage hardware. Watching the play from this high perch was always fascinating to me, particularly when the stage was full of people and the carefully choreographed stage business went off without a hitch, performance after performance. The whole evening was a vigorous assembly-line of efficiency, and each cog in the wheel appeared to be joyfully engaged, as if there was nothing else in the world they'd rather be doing at that exact moment.

Descending the iron staircase on my way to the basement of the theater where the wig room was set up, I was focused on the night ahead and happily mindful all my colleagues were as excited as I was. I had plenty of rehearsals behind me. I'd gone through a whole day in tech as Scrooge. I was ready. There was an atmosphere of studied calm in the building. The director couldn't have been more supportive and enthusiastic, and my "overstudy" had left a basket on the chair in his dressing room, a "Scrooge Survival Package" filled with cough drops, throat lozenges, herbal tea, and his favorite protein snacks.

The next two hours passed like a light snowfall: steady, serene, and calm. The machinery of this well-oiled production churned along. I hit all my marks and managed to enjoy myself, even allowing the occasionally stunning thought that I was here, in the flesh, dressed in Scrooge's clothes, saying Scrooge's lines, having Scrooge's thoughts, and sensing the stirrings of Scrooge's cold heart. When the time came for Scrooge to wake up on Christmas morning, redeemed and determined to be "as good a man as…the good old world knew," I felt as alive and grateful and close to tears as I'd ever been onstage, with more than a thousand people there to witness and share my joy.

And in the bat of an eye, it was over. Christmas passed into memory, and I was already in rehearsal for the next play, just as the trees were beginning to sprout spring buds, when I got a phone call. The role of Scrooge was mine.

I would get the chance to play the role every day, sometimes twice, for six weeks the following winter. How could it get any better than that?

But it did.

Chapter 56

EMILY'S CHRISTMAS CAROL

(Fall, 2000. "The Hub," Milwaukee Rep's common area. A spacious room with twenty-foot ceilings, and a wall of windows looking out over the Milwaukee River. Long tables with two-dozen chairs fill the space. Today the room is teeming with young children and their parents, who are filling out forms while their kids are busy silently mouthing the words as they read from identical pieces of paper.)

(The door to the rehearsal swings open, and the stage manager secures the doorstop with her foot. A half-dozen actors emerge, flushed with perspiration, carrying wooden dowels standing in for swords. They have been rehearsing a fight scene. One of the actors, JON, sees the mob scene of children and heads straight for the extension phone mounted on the wall next to the employee kitchen. He pushes the buttons of his home phone number and waits for a response. Loud laughter and whooping ensue.)

JON

Hey, guys! How are you doing?

GALE

    (To EMILY)

    Emily, it's Daddy!

EMILY

    (Squealing with delight)

    DADDY!! I'M WINNING CHUTES AND LADDERS!!

JON

    Sounds like lots of fun over there!

GALE

    Oh, we've had a great afternoon! I dropped off Sam at the forensics
    meet, and then Emily and I had Froot Loops for lunch, and now
    we're playing Chutes and Ladders. We've both won a game, and now
    we're playing for the championship.

EMILY

    I'M WINNING, DADDY!

    *(GALE laughs. A rich, contented laugh. JON wonders how long it
    has been since she laughed like that and feels a rush of gratitude.)*

IT HAD BEEN A little over five years since Gale's life had been
turned upside down. She'd found a psychiatrist who had juggled her
pharmacological cocktails until a therapeutic balance was achieved,
and after several tries, she'd finally found a therapist that she trusted.
My life partner had scaled peaks and endured painful descents into
valleys of frustration. She fought for her mental health the way other
people struggle with cancer. Her journey had taught her to be aware
that circumstances could change in a heartbeat, that the medication that
served for months or even years could suddenly change. But on this day,
we were all riding a wave of good will.

JON

I don't want to interrupt your game, but I forgot until just a few minutes ago that children's auditions for *A Christmas Carol* are today....

GALE

Oh no, have we missed it?

EMILY

MISSED WHAT, MOMMY!

JON

Could you get here in half an hour?

GALE

Sure. I think we could. We're all dressed.

JON

Do you think she wants to?

GALE

What do you *think*?

JON

Would it be OK with you?

GALE

Of course!

EMILY

WHAT ARE YOU TALKING ABOUT, MOMMY?

GALE

Daddy wants to know if you want to try out for *A Christmas Carol*.

EMILY
CHRISTMAS CAROL! CHRISTMAS CAROL! YES! YES!

EMILY HAD BEEN DYING to be in a play ever since I directed her in a kindergarten class play. A more convincing troll in *Three Billy Goats Gruff* had seldom been portrayed.

(Rehearsal hall, ninety minutes later. The door swings open again, the doorstop is secured, and JON hurries out the door to see EMILY, red bandanna on her head, white hoodie, blue jeans, and sneakers. GALE gives her husband a look, which the actor translates as "thanks for calling us...I think." JON is holding what looks like a bloody cauliflower in his hand, a rehearsal prop meant to suggest a severed head.)

EMILY
Can I watch your rehearsal, Daddy?

JON
(Hiding the prop behind his back)
No, not this one, kiddo. So how did it go?

GALE
It went very well, Daddy. The kids all sat in a circle and read their parts one after another. Emily was very relaxed and natural.

EMILY
I read the wrong line at first.

GALE
(To EMILY)
That's because there was a page missing from your script. Once that got cleared up, you did just fine.

(EMILY is beaming.)

JON

So, are you done?

GALE

Oh no. She read for one of the Cratchit kids, and now they want her to read for one of the Ghosts of Christmas Past. They're adding two children to be the ghost's helpers. They're going to take Scrooge by the hand and lead him through his past.

JON

(Hopeful)
Hey, does that mean Emily could be in the scene with me?

GALE

Well, you *are* Scrooge, aren't you?

(Ninety minutes later. The Hub is empty, all the kids have gone home. The door to the rehearsal hall opens again. Again, the sound of the doorstop shoved up under the door. JON emerges and walks over to his knapsack spread out on one of the chairs. He begins to pack up his things to go home. THE DIRECTOR of A Christmas Carol comes out of the adjoining rehearsal hall where he's been auditioning kids all afternoon. He is a tall, gray-haired man past middle age, but with the body of a man who looks like he bicycles thirty miles a week, which he does.)

THE DIRECTOR

Hey, man, how's it going?

JON

Great. We killed the king and stuck his head on a pike, so now we can all go home. How's it with you?

THE DIRECTOR

> Big day, big day. Lots of great kids. And I think I figured out how to end Act One.

JON

> Yeah?

THE DIRECTOR

> I don't want to give anything away until the actor agrees to play the role, but if it works out the way I hope it will, we're going to make you work.

> *(THE DIRECTOR walks away with a Cheshire-cat grin on his face.)*

AS I WAITED FOR the snail-like elevator, I thought, of all the hundreds of plays I've worked on in my career, all the great musicals, all the Shakespeare, my favorite had to be *A Christmas Carol*. I stood there and counted the reasons.

1. I love the story.

Dickens created a character that his readers could love to hate, a thoroughly hopeless case for humanity. And then he constructed a ghost story that scared the daylights out of them. Then he rescued his antihero from perdition by making him relive his past and making it possible for him to repair some of the damage he'd done in his sorry life. Who in the world can't relate to the idea of getting a second chance to atone for all the things you screwed up in the course of your time on earth?

2. I love the storytellers.

Actors, designers, directors, the people backstage who raise and lower two-ton set pieces, the woman who dabs rouge on the actors' cheeks, the parents who bring treats every day. And the kids! I love all of 'em, even the kid ten years ago in St. Louis whose feet smelled so bad that he cleared out an entire dressing room when he removed his barefoot shoes. Even the kid who threw a candle at another kid an hour before curtain and knocked out two of his teeth (fortunately, the father of one of the kids in the cast happened to be a dentist). Even the kid who turned ashen in the middle of a note session and projectile vomited, sending a dozen people scattering madly to avoid the collateral damage.

3. I love the rituals.

Everything from washing hands whenever offstage (in a futile attempt to stifle the petri dish of infection that runs through the cast and company multiple times each year), to group vocal warm-ups every day, to rounds of "Happy Birthday" sung just about nightly, to the Secret Santa drawing, to the Oops Jar where fines are paid whenever an adult slips up and utters an expletive of frustration. Even the production itself is its own ritual; four weeks spent preparing for Christmas by singing carols, trimming trees, and pretending to be invigorated by the cold while the temperature in the room rises to tropical extremes.

4. I love the machine.

A play spotted with crowd scenes, carefully choreographed to prevent anyone from being flattened by walls, scrims, and enormous flats. Scenes that take thirty seconds to perform and ten hours to stage. Scores of children, acting apprentices, and hardened professionals all working together to execute massive compositions of stage movement that look almost improvised, and half-a-dozen production assistants scurrying about on the fringes, invisible to the audience, shifting furniture, taking props from actors as they leave a scene, putting props in the hands of actors as they enter, making sure that the youngest actors don't get trampled by all the organized chaos.

And now, as I celebrated my fifth year in this glorious production, Emily turned nine and joined the party.

She was indeed cast as one of Christmas Past's "ghosties." Her first assignment was to walk onstage to the strains of entrance music, all alone, and stop center stage, where a special lighting cue revealed her. The location of the spotlight was set in stone. It wasn't a guy on a follow-spot. She had to hit her mark just in time for the last note of the music to resolve.

On the first run-through in the rehearsal hall, she hit her spot dead on. What a pro.

During that rehearsal, we were running the end of the first act for the first time. The various pieces of this elaborate puzzle had been staged and rehearsed, except for the closing moment. It was a flashback scene, where Scrooge was watching his younger self break up with the only love of his life. As Belle walked out of Scrooge's life forever, the entire cast assembled upstage, each of them holding a lit candle. When the musical cue played, the cast was to sing a five-part choral version of "O Come, O Come, Emmanuel," as Old Scrooge would slowly sink to the floor, heartbroken.

We'd never actually run through this part. Today was the day.

The cast was in position, their candles lit. The tape on which the musical accompaniment is recorded was cued up and ready. The adult Ghost of Christmas Past was poised and ready to speak his line. Everyone in the room waited for the cue to begin.

"Oh. Just one minute," the director broke in, holding up his hand. He loped up to Emily, knelt in front of her, and whispered something in her ear. Then he backed off just a little, still on his knees. He raised his eyebrows and murmured softly, "D'you understand?"

I watched her as she nodded.

"Okay. Let's run it."

I knelt on the floor; my rehearsal nightgown puddled around me. The Ghost of Christmas Past thundered, "These are the shadows of things that have been. That they are what they are, do not blame me."

The music began. And from the middle of the room, a single soprano voice, "O Come, O Come, Emanuel...."

Another voice joined, and then another. The director nodded toward Emily. She stepped forward and walked over to me. To Scrooge. To her dad. She knelt next to me. She reached up with her hand and touched my heart, just as the full company joined the hymn at its peak.

I hadn't known this was coming. I looked in her eyes. My daughter. The angel sent to me.

The music swelled. And so did my heart, to bursting. My eyes filled with tears. The script called for Scrooge to be sobbing.

I was already there.

The music ended. Silence filled the room. I couldn't move. I was exhausted from the hard work of running the act and overwhelmed by what had just happened. After a few moments I raised my head, and I could see that the floor below me was streaked with tears. I looked up at the actors with their candles. They were crying too.

I looked into Emily's brown eyes, at her angelic face wrapped in repose. I let the moment roll over me. I wanted to stay there, forever. It was a moment, *our* moment.

I looked up at the director. He was smiling. "I *told* you we were going to make you work."

Chapter 57

HEAD OF GOLD, FEET OF CLAY

ONE OF THE FEW disadvantages of my new life was that I had exchanged year-round employment in California for no more than six months work in Milwaukee. To pay the bills, I had to hit the road.

(2001. The expansive lobby of a performing-arts complex in central Illinois. An impeccably dressed, stylishly moussed woman with bright burgundy fingernails and matching lipstick is conducting an interview with JON. They sit facing each other on identical Naugahyde club chairs. She is the chair of the university theater department in whose facility they are meeting, but she is also the casting director of a notable Shakespeare festival out west. The interview is going well.)

CASTING DIRECTOR
　　Well, you come highly recommended by one of our guest directors, and I trust him. So, we'll just pass on you having to do audition pieces or anything and just get right to it.

JON
　　That's wonderful to hear. Thank you.

CASTING DIRECTOR

You'd be in three plays. Two of the directors know you, they've worked with you before. The third play is *King Lear*, where you'd play Edmund.

JON

That's wonderful! *(Bastard son, really bad guy, the kind of role I never get to play.)* Who's directing?

CASTING DIRECTOR

I'm sure you know him by reputation. He runs one of the top actor training programs in the country, and of course he wrote all those books.

JON

Acting for a Living? *That guy? The Dream Killer whose book I threw across the room when I was in college? The guy who said that having an acting career and a family is a hopeless ambition?*

(Smile in place, dying behind the eyes)
Gee…that's great.

IT WASN'T. FOR A guy who preached collaboration and "acting power" in his books, he turned out to be, in practice, a bullying impulse-killer.

On the first day of rehearsals, he announced that we all had to have all our lines memorized by the next day. We all had three plays to learn, and I imagined myself staying up all night just to accommodate him. I'd never worked with a director who made such a demand.

I had heard through the grapevine that his favorite teaching technique was literally lurking directly behind students, feeding inner monologues into their ear as they tried to concentrate during a scene. He abandoned this drill in rehearsals since there were seasoned professionals who would have probably decked him if he tried to inflict it upon them.

His directing style was about as inhibiting as anything I'd ever encountered. He told me when to move and where to look. He'd give me line readings that he insisted I copy. I remember turning to look my scene partner in the eyes one day, when he suddenly barked, "No! Don't look at her. She's not worth your attention." Was he talking about the character or the actor? Ultimately, his pompous misogyny over the next month convinced me that it was the latter.

The only consolation that kept me from having a creative meltdown was the knowledge that he directed *everybody* this way. Except for the actor playing Lear, a Method actor who was all impulse and no technique and who possessed a hot temper to boot. Our director let *him* get away with anything. There was the rehearsal when Lear grabbed his stage partner by the collar and flung him away as hard as he could. The young actor, who was a foot shorter and thirty pounds lighter than Mr. I-Do-What-I-Feel, hit the deck and was within inches of sliding into the seats offstage. To his endearing credit, the poor kid, a past student of mine who couldn't have been more than twenty, bolted up to his fifty-year-old colleague and screamed, "What the *fuck* are you doing, man? Don't you *ever* do that again!"

The Esteemed Director let the tension hang in the air for a minute before dictating, "Let's take a break." And then it was back to pontificating and inhibiting. I don't think I took a deep breath for a month.

On the Sunday after we opened *King Lear*, we were obliged to attend a dinner party at "the house my books built," his palatial, glass-enclosed hideaway nestled in the mountains. By this time, most of the actors had emerged from behind the thin curtains of generic pleasantries and were way past ingratiating themselves with His Highness. The play was open, we might never see this guy again if we were lucky, and we no longer had to protect ourselves by steadfastly observing *Rules for Actors, Rule #16: Bad directors always look for a scapegoat to mask their own failures. Don't be the scapegoat.*

I stood on the wraparound balcony, looking out over the spectacular view of the hills, and my glance fell to the Esteemed Director, grilling hamburgers and hot dogs on his lavish outdoor barbecue range.

My mind was racing with daring thoughts. I thought that if I had any nerve, I'd walk right up to him right now and say, "Thanks, Professor, for trying so hard to kill my dreams when I was in college that I spent twenty years proving you wrong. I'm one of those actors that you said would never have the house and the marriage and the kids and a decent career. You were wrong, and I've proven it!"

I drained my third glass of wine and decided that if I didn't eat some food soon, I might just make an idiot of myself.

I approached the food table where the director was still flipping burgers. My thoughts felt a little slushy and I feared that once I put my tongue in motion it would unravel. I didn't want to back out now, but my muddled mind was daring me to say my peace.

"What can I get for you?" he asked.

"A hot dog would be great," I stammered.

I'd rather have a hamburger. Why did I say hot dog? This is not going to go well. I'm not going to say what I want to say.

"I enjoyed your books," I eked out, with servile defeat.

"Thank you," he said, with a blank look on his face. He didn't really care what I thought. "There's ketchup, mustard, and relish on the table over there."

Come on. Say something. Tell him about your kids. Tell him that Sam is an honor student on his way to being valedictorian of his senior class and Emily's already been in her first play. Tell him how Sam's a state champion in forensics, and Emily recited a speech she wrote in front of thousands of people at a Milwaukee Bucks game. She was on the Jumbotron, for God's sake. Tell him.

The Esteemed Director dropped the hot dog on my open roll. "Come back for seconds. There's plenty of food."

He fixed me with an easy grin that cost him nothing. I smiled back at him, looking at a vague spot just above his head, and then I drifted away to the bar.

I didn't score any points against him. But as the evening wore on, it occurred to me that I'd scored all the points I needed. With myself. That was enough.

Chapter 58

GOD HELP US, EVERYONE

EIGHT MONTHS LATER, I found myself heading west for another summer at the Shakespeare Festival. But this time it wasn't for any Shakespeare. I got cast as Captain Hook in *Peter Pan*.

Truth telling time: *Peter Pan* is lost on me.

I'd played Hook before, in a perfectly competent, smartly produced version. But it left me cold. Top four reasons:

1. I don't like the story.

I've never understood the appeal of a "boy who wouldn't grow up." The world is full of grown men who never figured out how to move on past the selfishness and vanity of boyhood. I don't know; girls seem to grow up, so why not boys? I came to adulthood at the same time as the Equal Rights Amendment. I spent my thirties embarrassed for my gender, and by the time I hit my forties, I really couldn't work up much enthusiasm for stories that celebrated frat-boy behavior.

2. I don't really care for that whole Tinkerbell thing.

You know that part of the story when Tinkerbell is near death and the audience, composed mostly of kids, is supposed to bring her back to life by putting their hands together and clapping? What if they don't want to applaud? What if the production hasn't done anything to make them want to do their part? Does Tinkerbell die? Nope, you just pretend that whatever bogus spell was cast on the audience happened to work. The whole thing seems to be built on a big lie.

3. The ultimate nightmare: actors FLYING.

Little kids no taller than a tricycle FLY. Pubescent girls FLY, their budding breasts strapped into stiff leather harnesses. Young adult boys FLY, their gonads crushed as they try to avoid crashing into phony fireplaces and walls. None of this is a good idea.

Kirby's Flying Ballet was the first company to make kids fly in the original 1905 production, and apparently the effect was so realistic that they had to issue warnings to audiences along the lines of "don't try this at home." Nobody did it better than Kirby's.

By 1957, when Mary Martin played Peter in the Broadway musical version, an ingenious fellow named, appropriately, Peter (Foy), developed something called the Inter-Related Pendulum method. Foy built a business empire by renting his services to train backstage workers all over the world to use his system. It revolutionized stage flying. It was safe and painstakingly crafted and executed. Foy employees would come to a theater and train the technicians, and they wouldn't leave until they felt assured that the system was working and the backstage crew was thoroughly prepared.

Of course, there are ways around the system. Any unscrupulous producer can hire anybody who claims to know what they're doing. Just like anybody can write their own version of *Peter Pan*, because the rights are in the public domain. The 1905 script has lots of passages that now are considered misogynistic and racist, but like all theatrical chestnuts, at least it's benefited from thousands of productions where all the technical kinks have been worked out. That script is built like a Buick. And J. M. Barrie donated all his royalties in perpetuity to the Great Ormond Street Hospital Charity, the largest center for children's heart surgery in the United Kingdom. So, if you stick to the original script and you hire the Foys for the flying sequences, you're on your way and contributing to a good cause too. All you need is a good director to oversee the whole boondoggle. Lacking that spells trouble.

And finally…

4. There are all the impossible scene changes. I don't like those either. From the Darlings' bedroom to the High Seas to Neverland to the Darlings' again to the Lost Boys' hideaway and back to the Darlings'. Who in the world can pull that off? Without good planning and major technical support, a production of *Peter Pan* can stumble and lurch around like a drunken pirate on a three-day bender.

(2003. JON is on the telephone, listening to a pitch provided by an enthusiastic TALKING HEAD, otherwise known as the business manager.)

TALKING HEAD

We so hope you'll be joining us. It's going to be so special.

JON

(Married with two kids, needing the job)
I'm delighted you called.

TALKING HEAD

I think our new take on the story is going to be wonderful.

JON

(Feeling his heart stop for a second)
New take?
What kind of new take?

TALKING HEAD

We're writing our own adaptation. A world premiere.

JON

Who's writing it?

TALKING HEAD

Our director!

THE DIRECTOR. HE'S ALSO the producer of the theater. He's never written a play, as far as I know. He's wearing three hats. All at the same time.

This would have been a good time to bail out. Three hats make three huge red flags. But I ignored them. This was my first mistake of many to come.

Rules for Actors, Rule #17: Always follow your gut. Especially if it's churning.

JON
(Addressing his number-one fear)
What about the flying? Are the Foys going to be doing that?

TALKING HEAD
Oh no. Someone just as good. They work in *Las Vegas.*

(The red flags double in number, just like the crows on the jungle gym in The Birds. *"Get out! Get out while you can!" implore the voices in JON's head. The phone call ends. JON hangs up and wonders what he's gotten himself into.)*

A FEW WEEKS LATER, the script arrived at my door. I hoped that my reservations might be ameliorated by a thoughtful first reading. But when the first character to speak turned out to be Tinkerbell (to be portrayed by a fluttering pink light bouncing off the walls of the theater), things didn't look good. Especially when Tinkerbell spoke in the condescending tones of the most odious "children's theater" narrator. Will an actor be playing this role? Will it be a recorded voiceover? Can you teach a pink beam of light to talk? And who in the world could speak these words without gagging?

TINKERBELL
Oh dear! Oh dear! Hurry, children! Find your seats.

THE PLAYWRIGHT/DIRECTOR/PRODUCER is apparently imagining dozens of rosy-faced cherubs wandering about the auditorium, while the parents who drove them there stand in the aisles, all of them befuddled and not knowing how to proceed.

TINKERBELL

The STORY is about to begin! Oh, I do love a good STORY! Don't you just LOVE a STORY? And I'm IN this story! Can you believe it? A STORY is always a much better STORY when you're in it. OH! Please take your seats for this STORY! It's STORY telling time!

HERE IS WHERE THE children are to settle in, doomed never to rise again until the end of the STORY.

Maybe the table read will go better, I tell myself. And with the lights. And the costumes…

(One month later. The company is assembled in an abandoned middle school that should have been torn down thirty years ago. The PLAYWRIGHT/DIRECTOR/PRODUCER rises from his chair, removing all three of his hats. With his eyes glistening with tears, he takes a moment to collect himself and then begins to tell a tale from his own childhood.)

P/D/P

When I was a child, I knew how to fly. Every night. From my own bed. I thought it was wonderful. I told my mother. She thought it was wonderful. I told my father. He said it was ridiculous. And I could never fly again.

I exchanged an anxious look with the woman playing Mrs. Darling. She was seated next to me and had already poked me in the shin with her foot several times. She looked me straight in the eyes and mouthed a variation of Dickens: "God help us, everyone."

I felt like a twelve-year-old kid locked in the car, strapped in by a seatbelt, and pulling out on the highway.

Just as in the summer before, we were committed to a rotating repertory schedule where the three plays we were all in opened on the same ridiculous weekend. That meant we had just under four weeks to rehearse this play, and after two weeks it became clear that we'd never be ready. We sketched in each wretched scene in the steam bath of a rehearsal hall, knowing full well that the spit would almost certainly hit the fan when we moved into the theater and confronted sets requiring complicated scene shifts, flying sequences staged by We Are Not Foy, Inc., and numerous quick costume changes not accounted for in the incomprehensible script.

J. M. Barrie said it best: "To die will be an awfully big adventure."

On the first day of the first technical rehearsal, I walked in to behold the actor playing Peter (the same actor who'd been nearly kicked offstage by King Lear the year before) suspended ten feet above the stage, spinning out of control across the length of the proscenium, until he turned and landed face-first into the back wall of the set with a resounding THUD. One of the side flats, propped up hastily with a stage brace, somehow stayed upright. The director chose this moment to present me with his latest idea:

"Instead of you jumping off the ship to your death, I think we should blow you off the poop deck with a cannon ball. We'll put you in a harness and fly you to your doom. What do you think?"

I THINK I NEVER should have taken this job.
On the first flight test, I wobbled and gyrated like a yo-yo before being hauled to safety. The second time, I flew way past the intended mark and ended up bouncing off the back wall of the theater, bracing

myself by grabbing on to the EXIT sign. The third time, I found myself face-to-face with the counterweight system, narrowly missing a whole bank of stage lights.

But opening night was the best. I twisted around end to end like a poorly kicked field goal attempt and then hovered suspended in the air while the stage crew struggled to untangle the ropes. I was supposed to land quickly so I could make a prompt change and enter the next scene as Mr. Darling. As I seesawed over the stage like a sweaty Goodyear blimp, the actors below, having run out of scripted lines, ad libbed awkwardly as the stage crew hauled me in. Eventually I slid onto the stage, dripping with sweat, half dressed, looking a bit like Mr. Darling had been caught in flagrante delicto. One of the kids made a valiant try by offering how happy he was to be back home, and I breathlessly agreed. For me, leaving Neverland was the highlight of the night, because it meant the play was almost over.

We struggled through the final scene, and then the epilogue, and then we tiptoed apologetically through a hastily staged curtain call, hoping we'd get through the bows before the underwhelmed audience ran out of the will to clap for us.

The curtain wrung down slowly, tortoise-like, and when the chains at the bottom of the folds of fabric clanked quietly on the stage floor, Mrs. Darling/Tiger Lily took my hand. "We made it," she said, a brave smile on her face. We strode off the stage arm in arm, forever bonded by theatrical adversity. I opened the door to the stairwell that led down to the dressing rooms. She edged past me, lifting her massive skirts so she could negotiate the stairs. As we descended, one of the burly stagehands, clad in the traditional black, bellowed his gallows-greeting: "Only forty-two more shows to go!"

Peter Pan was our problem now. The perpetrators of this disaster moved on to other things, and the actors and crew were left holding the bag. We spent forty-two shows trying to fend off disaster by making up for the negligence, the mistakes, and the miscalculations—and hoping at the least that nobody would get hurt.

I almost made it.

On the last performance, while rushing in the dark to make that final entrance as Mr. Darling, I ran square into a six-inch platform that was out of its customary position, went head over heels, and sprawled across the floor, banging my head against the concrete. I scrambled to my feet and made the entrance on time, but my head was throbbing so badly that my mind went blank.

Dear Mrs. Darling took my arm, spoke my last line, and never left my side, through the final moments, through the epilogue, through the curtain call. It was over. Finally, unquestionably over.

On the morning after that last performance, Gale and the kids set out in our van for the long drive back to Milwaukee. But I still had a month or more of work to do. I had accepted an offer to direct the first production of the Shakespeare Festival's fall season. It was easy money and it meant that I'd be employed right up to my first day back in Milwaukee at the Rep, so I took it.

But as my family pulled away and I climbed the concrete steps to my barren apartment, now rendered sterile and grim and even sordid, I started to cry. The tears weren't tender or fanciful. They were angry. I raged around the room. I wanted to pound on the paper-thin walls. I wanted to scream out my resentment. I didn't care if the neighbors heard me.

This isn't worth it.

Five months away from Milwaukee. One month out of six with my family.

I'm not going to let this happen again.

Chapter 59

OVERNIGHT SUCCESS

I DIDN'T EXPECT THE world to come rolling to a stop to commemorate the day that I turned fifty.

And the world didn't let me down.

I had a two-show day at the Rep. Sam and Emily both had school. And Gale had college classes to teach forty miles away.

I was greeted in the early morning by the usual birthday ritual in our house: being pummeled by a dozen balloons as I lay sleeping. Emily, now eleven years old, took me by the hand and sat me down at the kitchen table.

It seems like all the significant events in my family's life have taken place at the kitchen table. Hurried lunch packing before school, platefuls of pancakes on Saturday mornings, confounding clashes with new math just before dinner, wrap-ups of the day over ice cream.

On the first morning of my fifties, my kids served me my favorite cereal and deluged me with crayon drawings (even Sam, who was now seventeen but thankfully not beyond such things), a few sneak-preview presents (the big opening would happen in my ninety-minute break between performances later), and a note signed by the kids and by Gale. It said, "Didn't know what to get you for your birthday until you said all you wanted was some cold hard cash. So, look in the freezer."

I stood up, opened the freezer door, and discovered a huge glass casserole dish with hundreds of pennies encased in a block of ice. They all dissolved into delighted guffaws. I was amazed how they had pulled off such a stunt without me noticing, and I was delighted to hear them all laughing and cheering. The last six years had included some hard times, but we'd never been so happy.

The clock was ticking, though, and we all had places to be. As I went out the door with the kids, Gale said to me (as if I needed a reminder), "Hurry home! We've only got an hour between shows and Birthday Fest has only just begun!"

Five o'clock brought a quick dinner so we could concentrate on the important stuff: presents. Nothing ostentatious, all of it thoughtful and "just what I wanted." And then, generous helpings of ice cream and cake. Even with a couple of cups of coffee for the road, I still had twenty minutes before I had to leave.

"There's something I've been meaning to tell you," Sam announced. "About college."

"You're skipping it and going straight into graduate school?" I deadpanned.

"No," he blushed. I think he could sense that I had a Big Brag coming on.

"Sam," I crowed, "do you remember that first parent–teacher conference when you were in ninth grade and your history teacher said she wished you could skip high school and just go straight to college?"

"I wasn't ready then," he demurred.

"I'm glad you stuck around," I admitted. "Even when that boarding school out east offered you a free ride."

"*I* wasn't ready for that," Gale piped up.

Sam put the conversation back on track. "I just want you to know that I want to go east to an Ivy League school. I know the tuition is really steep, and I know you can't afford it."

Ouch. The truth hurts.

"But you're not going to have to pay for this," he continued. "I'm going to do it on my own."

With a 4.0 average and a couple of state crowns in forensics and debate, a free ride from one of those schools was not out of the question. Once they looked at my annual income from being an actor, I figured his chances might just improve.

"I just want to make sure it'll be OK with you if I end up on the East Coast. I'm kind of hoping for Columbia."

Gale assured him. "I've known for a long time that you really want to live in New York City. And you're not the first one of our kids who almost ended up there. Right, Emily?"

Emily perked up and undraped a smile that revealed every single tooth.

I thought back to the afternoon I sat at a talent agency in Milwaukee, watching my daughter on camera, reading for a part in a feature film. There was a national search to find a kid to play Richard Gere's daughter in a movie, and our local agency had submitted Emily.

"I've never seen anybody her age with such presence," the casting agent gushed. "Look at her! The camera loves her. She looks like a little Juliette Binoche."

Not having seen a movie for adults since about 1986, I didn't know what that meant for Emily.

"They just cast the role of the mother opposite Richard Gere!" the agent continued. "You know who they signed? JULIETTE BINOCHE!"

The casting agent pulled up a photo of Juliette Binoche from the internet and showed it to me. She looked just like Emily, all grown up.

Eventually, the producers flew Emily and her mom out to New York City for a face-to-face audition. The field was narrowed down to two girls. The other girl got it.

That was as close as we'd got to New York ever since the guy in the three-piece suit had taken the rotten egg in the head that should have been meant for me.

"Sam," I promised, "you can go anywhere you want. You're ready for anything."

Then I grabbed one last scoop of ice cream, thanked my family for a wonderful birthday, and hurried out the door for the drive downtown.

I got to the theater barely a half hour before curtain. That was all the time I needed. It was a small role, a character who didn't come on for the first hour. One of those "plot device" characters who comes in with a little information that moves the story forward and then disappears until the very end for curtain call. I'd been playing quite a few of those roles lately, to the point that I was relating my frustration to that of the utility infielder who comes in for a few innings and then yields to a heavy hitter when the team needs a power surge late in the game. "I don't know why they don't give you more to do around here" had become a phrase that I was tired of hearing.

But I'd just had a meeting with Joe Hanreddy, the Rep's artistic director and, as we say these days in employee-relations circles, my "supervisor." It's true that, over the years, I had wished for bigger roles and more responsibilities, but he was unerringly loyal to me for a solid dozen years, making sure that I was on contract for at least thirty weeks a season. And now he offered me some of the deepest, richest roles I'd had in several years. I'd have more than enough chances to have some quality at-bats in the starting lineup.

And then there was Winona. As in Minnesota. The Great River Shakespeare Festival had been founded in 2004 by a group of directors including my lifelong mentor, Paul Barnes, a guy I'd known since our California days when he arrived in Santa Maria just as we thought I was on my way out. He understood my desire to raise a family amid the demands of a life in the theater, and his support made it happen. He invited me to be in his first season at Great River, and for the next decade he gave me the chance to play some of the greatest Shakespearean roles of my career: Richard III, Bottom, Shylock, Malvolio, Prospero, Falstaff, King Lear. Thanks to him and the Rep, I spent a decade employed for almost fifty weeks out of every year. That was job security that most actors could only dream of.

I had everything I'd wanted. Steady work. Talented, loving kids. A devoted wife who had rebuilt her life after emotional turmoil and personal loss.

I looked at myself in the mirror.

I noticed a bald spot on the top of my head, which I swear hadn't been there the day before. I took a long hard look at the hair that remained. It had been silver, but now it was turning white. I still looked pretty good for fifty.

Fifty.

I thought back to that steamy, gin-laced afternoon thirty years ago, when Mikey and I sat at a rickety kitchen table in Madison, and he read my tarot. "You'll be an overnight success," he had predicted, "at fifty."

Damned if he wasn't right.

Chapter 60

THE READINESS IS ALL

EIGHT YEARS LATER, IN 2012, I found myself seated at the same makeup table at the Rep where I'd noticed my bald spot. I took one last look at my reflection in the mirror, stood up, pushed my chair into the table, and checked myself in the three-quarter-length mirror. My earth-tone tie with the faint yellow contours was tied in a thin knot, straightened, and carefully fitted to cover the top button of my light-gray shirt. I gave the vest of my suit a deft tuck, erasing whatever fold may have set in as I was sitting. The shoulders of my suit coat had been brushed free of whatever lint or dandruff may have accumulated. I inspected the crease in my newly pressed pants. Attention to detail was important to Otto, or at least the Otto I was creating.

I turned my back on the mirror so I could swing around and sweep my outer coat off the wooden hanger. I shot my arms smoothly down the inner sleeves, first the right arm, then the left. I faced the mirror and adjusted the lapel of my coat, so the yellow Star of David sewn on to the chest was clearly visible. Even though I was just an actor wearing a costume, the sight of that badge sent a chill up my spine every time I looked at it.

I rustled the back of the collar and raised it a few inches above my neck, making sure it landed neatly over my suit collar, just like my dad taught me to do all those years ago when we walked into church on Sunday morning. My dad's maddening attention to detail was serving me now.

The final touch was the homburg, aligned gently on top of my head, covering my razor-thin haircut. I turned one last time to face the mirror. My makeup was subtle; in a five-hundred-seat house, a thrust stage configuration where the audiences on the side were close, not much amplification of features was needed. Besides, I had plenty of creases and wrinkles of my own. I had earned every single one of them over the years. My one concession was a sallow base and shadowy texture around the eyes, meant to convey the afflicted look of a man who has been trapped indoors for a much longer time than is healthy.

I turned off the makeup lights, stepped into the carpeted hallway, and eased the door shut. I walked to the end of the hallway, glancing at my reflection in the full-length mirror. A cheerful young woman wearing a brightly colored smock stepped in my path. Pushing the pencil in her hand into her Brillo pad of bright-red hair, she looked me over, adjusted my tie, and chirped, "You look great. Have a good show."

"Thank you, Melanie," I murmured a little distractedly, just as a voice came over the speaker, "Ten minutes to places, please, ten minutes." I was a little early for call, as I was every day for this play. I needed at least five minutes of quiet meditation before this one.

Grabbing the steel handrail, I slowly descended the first six steps. To the left was the door that led to the theater balcony. Six more steps took me to a landing between floors. Another six steps and the door to the orchestra section was on my right. Six more steps took me to stage level. But I kept going, down another six steps, then a slight turn, and then eight more steps. It was a long way down, and with every flight, my breathing deepened. I checked my jaw for any excess tension. The challenge over the next two hours was to stay relaxed.

The room under the stage was dimly lit, just illuminated enough so I could find my chair. I sat down next to the actor who was playing my wife Edith. We'd shared hundreds of performances over the years, laughing and wisecracking backstage. On this day, we nodded to each other in silence.

When I heard a certain lilt in the flute solo in the prerecorded music, I stood up and walked to the foot of the wooden stairs that I would soon climb to reach the stage. I looked around the cramped chamber that was visible only to the audience seated in the balcony. The space had been designed to look like a cellar. The walls were lined with dusty bottles of wine, canned vegetables, rusted workshop equipment, and a small valise containing samples of spices from Otto's days as a salesman, when he worked hard to make a good living for his family, back before everything changed and they went into hiding. The monogram engraved into the leather read "O. H. F."

No one would ever see these details except me and Jim Guy, the props artisan who designed it. Jim had performed his usual exquisite observance of period detail. More than any other props designer I had known, he lived to create a world that would stimulate the actors' imaginations, transporting all of us, audience included, to a warehouse/office building in 1942 Amsterdam.

Otto reached the top step, now in full view of witnesses to the story, and paused to take in a panoramic view of the last place his family ever gathered. It seemed larger. His footsteps echoed emptily as he stepped into the "living room," or rather, the 9'x11' box that served as the center of activity in those long-ago months.

Familiar objects came into focus, as Otto took in the scene guardedly. The teacup that his daughter Margot drank from every morning, its dregs dried up and turned to dust, a spoon still resting on the mismatched saucer. The wooden carton, stained a metallic black, still holding the matches that Otto used to light his pipe at night, until there was no more tobacco to be smuggled in. The iron water pitchers were still standing in the sink, their wide spouts and rounded chambers ideally suited for a purpose for which they were never intended: the toilets couldn't be flushed during daylight hours, for fear of arousing suspicion among the warehouse workers on the first floor, so the jugs served as chamber pots for the eight occupants.

Otto moved through the room somberly, measuredly, determined to remain steady, composed. But then he stopped in front of the bed. Their bed. The bed he shared with Edith. Her meager sewing kit lay open, its contents splayed rudely on the beaded quilt. A threadbare green sock belonging to his younger daughter Anne, a dangling piece of thread still connected to the needle buried amid the scattered spools. There had been no time to restore the contents before all eight of them had been rounded up and pushed down the stairs and into the street. Otto sat on the bed, his legs having given out under him. He was surprised and rendered helpless by the storm rising from his chest. Before he could summon up any defense, he was sobbing, tears rushing down his cheeks and spilling on to the beads of the quilt. A wailing moan emerged from him. The hollow, anguished bellow filled the room.

That was the beginning of my workday, every day, for five weeks. And twice on Saturdays and Sundays.

It was my responsibility, my privilege, to play Otto in *The Diary of Anne Frank.*

Chapter 61

ROUGH MAGIC

THE DIARY OF ANNE FRANK was one of the most emotionally demanding, solemn experiences I'd ever had in the theater. It was my job, with the help of the other actors, the stagehands, the director, and the designers, to remind the audience that we human beings are capable of inflicting barbarous atrocities on each other.

I'd start thinking about the play two hours before getting in the car to drive downtown. I needed all the preparation possible so I could do the play justice. But it was also stressful living in that world for two solid months, and I relied on getting in a good physical workout on performance days. I did calisthenics in the dressing room before every show. I did deep breathing exercises and I meditated for ten minutes at the half-hour call. And every other day, I relied on running to keep me active.

One morning, a few hours before a matinee, I dressed in running clothes suitable for the unseasonably cold weather: stocking cap, gloves, and a thermal jersey under my T-shirt. I was lacing up my running shoes when Emily walked into the kitchen. It was a day of parent–teacher conferences, so she had the day off from her junior year of high school.

Normally, I liked to run alone, because I moved at a leisurely pace and I didn't like to struggle to keep up with a jogging partner, but Emily liked to jog unhurriedly like me. In fact, she'd decided to forgo returning to the cross-country team because keeping up with the rest of the team was such a frustrating ordeal.

I invited her to come along. I chose a three-mile course, nothing too strenuous. It started at our front door, and the halfway point was the cemetery where we'd buried my dad a quarter century before. I'd only managed a visit or two over the years until 2006, when Mom joined him there. From that point on, it had become a monthly stop on my running routine.

Emily and I set out at a nicely manageable pace, our breaths visible in the cold air. Soon we arrived at my parents' graves, and as we stood under the maple tree that offered them shade in the summer, I said a silent prayer. Then, as Emily drifted off to give me a few moments to myself, I filled in the folks about what was going on in my life. This visit was a lot like what they had been when my parents were alive: me talking mostly to Mom because I was confident she was listening, and Dad quietly witnessing, wandering in and out of my attention. After all these years, it was Mom who I needed to see. I missed her every single day.

After a few minutes, we began our jog toward home. As I stepped toward the gravel-tossed curb just outside the cemetery's front gate, I felt a sharp pain in my foot. Damn. I hobbled over to the bus stop on the corner, propped myself up against the pole, and raised my left leg so I could see the bottom of my shoe. A nail was sticking out of the rubber tread mark. I untied the shoe and took it off. The nail dislodged itself from my foot, and now there was blood. A lot of blood, dripping onto the pavement.

Emily, who inherited my squeamishness about such sights, was torn between looking away so she wouldn't faint, and wanting to help. I quickly thought of a way that both her responses could be of practical use.

"Why don't you run home and tell Mommy to get in the car and meet me here?" I suggested.

"Are you sure?" Emily asked, noticeably relieved that she wouldn't have to stand there and watch me bleed.

"Don't worry, I'm fine," I assured her. "I'll just wait right here for you. See? I've already stopped bleeding. Look."

Emily took my word for it, favored me with a concerned look, and set out on a jog across the street.

Watching her, I could see that she ran just like me and I wondered. How had she gotten so tall?

I sat on the concrete disk that housed the cemetery's entryway monument, and I waited, trying to ignore the growing anxiety that this injury might cut down on the hour I liked to arrive before curtain. After about twenty minutes, Gale and Emily pulled up. I crumpled with an inelegant thud into the front seat, and we raced to the emergency room, less than half an hour away.

(Ten minutes later. Emergency room lobby. JON hears his name called, limps down the hall, and steps into an examination room. GALE and EMILY stay behind in the lobby. JON waits another fifteen minutes. A cheerful, anonymous doctor draws the curtains and bustles in.)

DOCTOR

Hi there! I hear you've stepped on a nail. Oww! That must hurt—

JON

I hope this doesn't take long, Doctor. I've got to be downtown soon. It's really important.

DOCTOR

Well, let's see what we've got here.... Oh yeah, that looks deep. We'll clean you up, give you a nice thick bandage, and you'll be on your way. I've got your records here, and I don't see any evidence of a tetanus shot in the last ten years. So we better give you one just in case. It might take a few more minutes, is that OK?

(JON looks at his watch. One hour before curtain. Still time to drive downtown if the traffic's light.)

JON

Sure. As long as I'm out of here in a few minutes.

(Minutes pass. A lot of minutes. A NURSE arrives with a large needle. She unwraps JON's foot, cleans it thoroughly, then injects the needle.)

Ouch. That hurts. OK. Bandage on. Shoe fits over it. Walking hurts, but I can do it. Take a deep breath. Gonna make it.

(Moments later. Lobby. GALE and EMILY walk up to JON. GALE wears a hesitant look.)

JON
> OK, let's go.

GALE
> I need you to stay calm. Do you promise to me that you'll stay calm?

JON
> Why? What's going on?

GALE
> Your stage manager called. Did you know that the curtain today is at one thirty?

JON
> No, it's at two.

GALE
> No, it's at one thirty. That's ten minutes from now. We're a half-hour away.

(JON stops breathing for just a minute.)

GALE
> Your understudy's going on.

JON

THE HELL HE IS!

(The handful of people in the lobby look up.)

We can be there in ten minutes. They'll hold the curtain.

GALE

It's too late. They can handle it. Let the understudy go on. This is why they *have* understudies.

JON

(Exploding)
No! I am not going to miss this. Let's get in the car—now.

GALE

But it's almost—

JON

NOW!!!

(EMILY jumps a foot. JON is out the door.)

(Inside the car. Three minutes and seventeen seconds later. GALE is pulling out into traffic.)

JON

Can't you go any faster?

GALE

I could, but I'd rather not get arrested.

(EMILY speaks up from the backseat. She's holding GALE's phone and has been speaking to the stage manager.)

EMILY

She says they can hold the house for ten minutes, no more.

JON

(Growling like a caged animal)

We can make it if you drive FASTERRRR!

(GALE, a careful driver and scrupulous follower of the speed limit, is pushing seventy in a 55-mph zone. Either she cares a lot for JON or is afraid of him in his current frenzy.)

EIGHT MINUTES LATER, we pulled up to the theater. I flung open the stage door and sprinted past the understudy who was pacing and reciting lines under his breath.

I had four minutes to get ready.

Melanie had laid out my costume on the first floor, eight steps away from the door leading to the trap room under the stage. I tore off my shirt, my running pants, my shoes. I pulled on Otto's pajamas, underdressed for the second scene. The gray shirt. The brown tie. The pants. The vest. The coat. The overcoat. The homburg. Melanie gave me a quick inspection and nodded. I raced down the steps to the trap room, scurrying past the other actors. The flute solo reached the spot where I enter. I dashed to the bottom of the stairs. My heart was beating through my layers of clothes, my head throbbing with urgency and waves of sun-drenched images: The freeway. Our car flying past everybody else. The emergency room doctor. The cemetery. My shoe full of blood.

I took a breath, and the images disappeared, like an extinguished candle. My one hour of preparation reduced to a moment, to a second.

I trudged up the stairs. I saw the teacup, the match box, the water jugs. I stopped at the bed. I picked up the green sock. And Otto's legs caved in at the knees. The storm rose in his chest. The sobs and moans and bellows filled the room.

There was no time for the flood of trivial thoughts that often dance in and out of my consciousness when I'm trying to live in the moment onstage. My brain and heart had no room for grocery lists, middling anxieties, or remnants of conversations started backstage. It was in that moment, as I walked into 1942 Amsterdam without time to prepare, that I experienced the moment of transformation that as an actor I had spent my whole life trying to find. It was like I was some kind of emotional chameleon, stepping onto a leaf spattered with strains of gold and red and green, with the colors of my scales changing immediately to blend into the surroundings. The bleeding runner with a hole in his foot disappeared into the shadows, and Otto Frank emerged.

Forty-five years earlier, I'd experienced this sensation for the first time.

On that cold, rainy day in January of 1964, I was dressed in the first real costume I'd ever worn, the black robe buttoned halfway to the floor, laced with the faint scent of boys who had worn it before me; ironed white chasuble flared with flowing sleeves reaching just beyond the elbow, all of it layered over my blue button-down shirt and green corduroys. I felt special, part of something important. I was an altar boy. It was the 10:00 a.m. Sunday Mass.

I stepped off the linoleum floor, and the sound of my footfalls disappeared into the thick green carpet. I raised the gold candlelighter with both hands until the lit wick illuminated each candle, and the church began to fill with the scent of scorched leaves and rancid oil. I was standing in God's house now, a place where the ennui of my boy's life was suspended, and nothing mattered except the sacred reality of the Mass. I watched spellbound as Father Petta, a balding, stoop-shouldered man, turned bread and wine into body and blood, emboldened by the God with whom I shared this holy space. I watched Father Petta turn the palms of his hands upward, then bend at the waist and kiss the altar, then raise himself to a height far beyond his normal reach, lifting the ciborium above his head as I rang the silver handbell with vigor.

I lived in these moments fully, not as a prepubescent child of God, but as an ordinary kid transformed by ritual, by the intrinsic belief that what I was caught up in, at this exact moment in time, was life to its fullest point, at its most compelling capacity. I was swept out of the ordinary and carried away to something deep and sacred. My belief in Catholic orthodoxy would fade away as soon as I entered adulthood, but my faith in the power of ritual was imprinted that day.

That's what I experienced on that remarkable afternoon in the Annex, in our imaginary world of 1942 Amsterdam. That sense of belief in the illusion I was helping to create, and the selfless ability to step into another man's shoes and tell his story, so people sitting a few feet away in a dark theater could be transported too. I could invite them along, and if they took the journey with me, they would be moved, and maybe even changed.

It's a damn good way to make a living, and as I edged closer and closer to what I had been taught was retirement age, I pledged to myself that I'd be acting until I drew my last breath. Even after I started collecting social security checks and drawing on my pension, I'd still be acting. Retirement was for people who hated their jobs and couldn't wait to be done with them. And if I was truly lucky, I'd be one of those actors who would die onstage. One night I'd be in the middle of some high-flying monologue or locked in some high-stakes fireworks with a brilliant actor in some magnificent play, in the kind of role I'd always wanted to play, and off I'd go. I'd get to the overstuffed chair in time, sinking into the cushions, closing my eyes.

The rest is silence.

EPILOGUE

IN FIFTY YEARS (INCLUDING college and community theater), I've only missed four performances. I can still count 'em on one hand.

The first time was the night my father died.

The second time, twenty years later, I was so sick that I couldn't get out of bed.

The third time was the night Gale had a heart attack.

And the fourth time was the dress rehearsal when I took a twelve-foot dive down an open trapdoor to a concrete basement. Stage carpenters had to dismantle the escape stairs to the trap room with a buzz saw so the paramedics could get to me. My understudy went on for previews.

But I made it back in time for opening night, bounding about the stage, playing the part of a ten-year-old boy while the pain shot through my body like a lit string of cherry bombs.

I've had to leave the stage in the middle of a scene to throw up in an offstage waste basket and then go right back on to finish the scene. I know a lot of actors who tell the same story. Two of my friends performed while undergoing chemotherapy for colon cancer, with colostomy bags strapped inside their costumes.

The show must go on.

And then came the ides of March 2020, when that cliché was exposed for the lie that it is. The show did not go on; in fact, it died overnight.

I spent my final moments in a theater watching my daughter, now a professional actor in her own right, run through a dress rehearsal of a play that never opened. Within days, every theater in America had closed its doors, forcing thousands of actors, designers, directors, and technicians out of work.

There were consolations. Emily ended up staying home with us for four months because it wasn't safe for her to travel back to New York City. Sam, who not only made it to the Ivy League but earned a PhD and became a professor of history, came home when his campus shut down, and stayed with us for the next six months. With our family reunited in this bizarre, once-in-a-lifetime twist of fate, we got to pick up where we had left off when our kids had flown the coop years before. Meanwhile, my first social security check arrived, and I toppled harmlessly into a safety net like an acrobat slipping off a swing.

As I pondered how to pass the time during a shutdown that all of us expected to last a few weeks, I sat down to begin this book.

I wanted to make some sense out of this never-boring fun-house amusement that was my career. How did this offbeat profession I chose relate to the story of my life? The question that I'd been trying to answer all these years was still toying with me: "If I'm not an actor, who am I?" Here was my chance to answer that question once and for all.

For twenty months I absorbed myself in the task of rereading my journals, assembling a coherent narrative of my career, and reliving happy memories while enduring painful ones.

The walls of the room in which I've worked are dotted with the mementos of my life. There is very little visual evidence that an actor occupies this space. Newspaper articles written about me over the years, publicity interviews to which I've submitted, and theater programs containing my credits are all filed away in boxes. There are lots of photographs, but they're the kind of family memorabilia that most people favor: my wedding day. Afternoons at the beach with the kids. The day that my siblings and I got corralled long enough to pose for a studio portrait. My parents. Their parents.

On my desk is a newspaper photograph of an eight-year-old boy standing at a kitchen counter, munching a soda cracker. My fingers are wrapped around a tall glass of milk. I am posing self-consciously for a photographer. He is shooting a promotional spread of my parents' remodeled kitchen for the local paper.

It's been a long shoot and I'm tired. I'd rather be outside playing in the snow. I am years away from any awareness that someday I'd be earning my living making faces and speaking somebody else's words.

My memory sweeps the eight-year-old me out of the kitchen and deposits him safely at the wing-tipped feet of my father.

Dad touches his Viceroy to the Magic-Race flash paper, and the starter's flag ignites. The burning ember spreads to the first horse, then the second, and all the way down to the fifth horse.

But the flash paper is subject to the whims of its design. There are microscopic inconsistencies, little pieces of wood or dust floating about inside the grain. Sometimes the flame leaves the drawn line of the racing path and snuffs itself out. Seabiscuit comes up lame. Or Night Mare drifts into War Admiral's path, and both horses flame out. This is frustrating for me to watch, but the hard lesson is learned: sometimes it's not who finishes first, but simply who is still standing when the flame burns out.

The flame has glimmered within me for fifty years. So many of my friends and colleagues gave up on theater as a profession after ten years, or twenty, but I'm one of the lucky ones still standing, living on a gluttonous diet of survivor pride. So long as I'm fit and strong enough to endure the roller coaster ride of rehearsals, the happy torture of learning lines, and the nightly ritual of sharing the work with a roomful of people, who am I to quit?

But fate answers with an unimaginable plague, a shuttering of stagehouses the likes of which haven't been seen since the Renaissance. Comfortably ensconced in my living room, secure in my bubble, I live for almost two years without pretending to be somebody else. I could get used to this. The flame is flickering.

COVID protocols begin to ease. Theaters announce plans to reopen. And my phone rings. It's my hometown theater. I haven't been at the Rep in three years. They're doing a fun play guaranteed to be a crowd pleaser. A generous salary on top of my pension and social security. A good long run.

Fumbling my way through the dark, I strike a match and light the candle on my desk, the one I've been using for months to calm me down, to focus me as I write.

I stare into the blue-and-yellow blaze. It wavers weakly. For a moment it looks as if it's going to expire. And then it flares, turning a warm shade of gold and yellow.

I take the job.

So now I'm an actor again. The show is open, and it's as fun as I hoped it would be. I'm getting used to working until eleven o'clock every night.

But the blaze that used to rage through my soul has dimmed, reduced to a genial, insignificant little flame.

After almost two years of lockdown, I'm reminded of a lesson learned thirty-five years ago, on a windswept beach in California, with a newborn baby tucked under my coat: that acting is not who I *am*. It's simply what I *do*.

And then life throws me a curveball, an off-speed pitch on the inside corner, just when I'm looking the other way.

My doctor persuades me to undergo a physical after I've stayed away from hospitals and medical offices for twenty months.

One of the results of a blood test leads to an MRI, which leads to a biopsy. My doctor assures me that there's an eighty percent chance that I've got nothing to worry about. He tells me, "Let's wait for the results, and go from there."

The results come back. I am not one of the eighty percent.

I'm at a very low risk. This thing could lay dormant in my prostate for years.

But it's cancer.

There's no reason for me to doubt that I'm going to survive and even thrive with this diagnosis. I'll go in every few months like a good, compliant patient, and my newly designated medical team and I will monitor the situation.

I could even continue acting. I've got another job coming up just after the one I'm currently doing is over.

But a couple of weeks after my diagnosis, I dip into my thoughts.

In my mind's eye I survey the blue cavern that I've always imagined is the dwelling place of my soul. I sweep through the cave until I locate it. The flame. Is it still gleaming?

It's a cool shade of blue. Pretty, like the sky. But its days as a luminous guide have faded.

Let it go, it pulses quietly to me.

The next day, I turn down the job. I'll finish up the run of the play I'm doing, and for the first time in a very long time, I won't know what's coming next.

For a few days, a disconcerting void appears when I scan the cavern where my soul lives. But slowly I come to recognize that what's there is not a sense of vacancy or emptiness.

It's something rooted much deeper.

It's freedom.

For forty years I've taken every single acting job that's come along, even the ones I didn't really want to do.

I don't have to do that anymore.

When I share my thoughts with Gale, she says, half playfully, "Maybe you've finally decided to grow up."

I shudder at the thought. "Why do you think I wanted to be an actor? I *never* wanted to grow up."

"Peter Pan never wanted to grow up. I thought you hated Peter Pan."

Ouch.

Part of getting old is accepting that ambivalence isn't necessarily a sign that you're trying to bullshit yourself. Life is complicated. Maybe I'll find myself in a play again someday; I don't know. Like all vocations, the theater boasts a captivating call to action, but I hope that I'll be perfectly content to wait for something to come around that I really *want* to do, not one that I think I *ought* to do.

Today I am looking at the future as a rolling landscape, seen from a distant elevation, maybe one of those vistas I encountered years ago when I was driving through the mountains out west.

I imagine I've been hiking through a canyon all day, and now I'm heading home. A tourist's impulse invites me to pull off the road at one of the lookout points. I park my car and walk to the edge of a guardrail, looking back over my left shoulder at an earthly panorama of winding roads and rolling groves of trees. Each of these roads leads down a path that I can see here from the bluff, but I know that, when I was walking these paths just a few hours ago, I had no idea of where the trails were leading me. Did I enjoy the hike? Did I take extra care to relish the scenery all around me? Did I live in the moment, every step of the way? Of course not. Nonetheless, the view from the vista puts a lump in my throat. I have gratifying memories of the journey that has taken me this far.

Pebbles and stones scrape under my feet as I turn to look over my right shoulder. It's going to be a thrilling sunset. In the meantime, there are a whole new set of trails and paths stretched out before me. I could call it a day and return to my car, but there's plenty of time to squeeze in another hike before nightfall. I press the remote button to lock the car, and step off the smooth concrete, trudging through the trampled-down grass that leads to the trails.

As I walk further and further away from where I've been before, I take deep breaths and fill my lungs with the thin, dry air. All I can hear is the faint rustle of wind blowing through the canyon. And then the words of my favorite poet, Carl Sandburg, come to mind, teasing me, urging me, inviting me to keep moving:

The broken boulders by the road
Shall not commemorate my ruin.
Regret shall be the gravel under foot.

I can feel the gleaming sun bathing my back and shoulders. A new wave of energy flutters through my body.

I can't wait to see what I find at the next lookout.

CURTAIN CALL

RULES FOR ACTORS, RULE #18: When it comes time for you to take a bow, be gracious. And grateful.

Some actors hate curtain calls. They rebel against the awkwardness of a ritual that they consider outmoded, a relic of some earlier era. They hurry to center stage, suddenly embarrassed at all the attention; they look up at some vague spot somewhere in the ceiling, straining to smile because the director has exhorted them to "Have fun up there! You look like you're going to your own execution!" Then they hurry through an apologetic bow and scramble to the safety of the other actors assembled upstage.

I love curtain calls because they give me the chance to say:

Thanks for coming.

Thanks for listening.

Thanks for affirming that what I do has some value.

Thanks for encouraging and supporting me in this harrowing, extraordinary, seemingly endless, vulnerable, and gratifying adventure of putting my thoughts on paper.

Writing, just like acting, is such a collaborative labor. You can't do it by yourself, just as a solo performance is supported by a small army of backstage allies.

Cherie Kephart has taught me more about writing than I ever could have imagined. She is a brilliant developmental editor, a writer who practices what she preaches, and a good new friend. They're hard to find when you're pushing seventy.

Asa Wild has arranged my words into this graceful format that you hold in your hands. She is an artist, a collaborator, and a dear friend of nearly twenty years.

I am indebted to the real-life people who I refer to in this book as Mary Margaret, Anna, Mikey, and Terry. I have dipped into their personal lives to tell my story. Thank you for the joy you brought to my youth when I was so callow and stupid. I didn't appreciate you enough.

Gale, the light of my life, and Sam and Emily, three souls for whom I bear more love and admiration than any other humans who walk on this earth, have read my drafts repeatedly and have alternatively served as cheerleaders, constructive critics, and sources of constant inspiration.

This book is for them.

And to all the other characters who flit in and out of this book, I hope that I've told stories pretty much the way you remember them. I'm grateful to all of you for gifting my life with love, friendship, and good times.

My siblings should get a bow of their own for putting up with me all these years, and for their steadfast devotion to seeing me in plays, no matter how good or bad they were. My mom never wavered in her support of the profession I chose, and my dad at least didn't try to stop me. Ultimately, he inspired me to live up to his favorite motto: "To thine own self be true."

OK. Here I go. I may look like I'm doing this alone, but I carry all of you in my heart.

(2022. JON bounds onto the stage from the wings. He reaches center. He stands up straight, pulls his shoulders back, SMILES, takes a bow, waves, and exits.)

(Lights fade to black.)

ABOUT THE AUTHOR

JONATHAN GILLARD DALY has never been on Broadway, never been in a television series, and has never made a feature film. Instead, he has worked happily in the professional theater for 45 years.

Here's a partial list of theaters at which he's performed since he joined Actors' Equity Association in 1978: Madison Repertory Theater, Repertory Theatre of Saint Louis, Great Lakes Shakespeare Festival, Pacific Conservatory of the Performing Arts/Theaterfest, Body Politic Theater, Great River Shakespeare Festival, American Players Theater, Indiana Repertory Theater, Court Theatre at the University of Chicago, Cincinnati Playhouse in the Park, New Jersey Shakespeare Festival, Milwaukee Repertory Theater, and Utah Shakespeare Festival.

He is also the author of several plays, all of which have enjoyed professional productions: a musical memoir, *The Daly News*; a drama, *To The Promised Land*; and a solo play, *An Evening Of Carl Sandburg*.

He has been married for forty years to playwright Gale Childs Daly. They live in Milwaukee, Wisconsin.